STRAIGHT FROM THE HEART

♥

**Authors, Celebrities & Others
Share Their Philosophies on
Making a Difference in the World**

—♥—

by Danielle Marie

ALLWON
PUBLISHING CO.

ALLWON
PUBLISHING CO.

3000 Redhill Avenue
Costa Mesa, California 92626

Copyright 1992 by Danielle Marie. All rights reserved.
No part of this book may be used or reproduced without written permission except in the case of brief quotations for use in articles and reviews.

The excerpt from Jean Houston's *The Search for the Beloved* is reprinted by permission from Jeremy P. Tarcher, Inc., Los Angeles, California, © 1987.

The excerpt from Gerald Jampolsky's *Out of Darkness into the Light: A Journey of Inner Healing* is reprinted by permission from Bantam Books, New York, New York, © 1989.

All information in this book is given without guarantees on the part of the author or the publisher. This book is sold with the understanding that the statements expressed are not those of the author or publisher, and the author and publisher disclaim all liability in connection with the implementation of this information. Every effort has been made to make this book as authentic and accurate as possible. However, the publisher has retained the right to acknowledge the titles of all contributors in their biographies and edit where necessary in order to maintain the literary style intended.

Library of Congress Cataloging-in-Publication Data
Straight from the heart: authors, celebrities, and others share their
 philosophies on making a difference in the world / (compiled) by
Danielle Marie.
        p.   cm.
    Includes index.
    ISBN 1-880741-09-1 (acid-free paper)
    1. Conduct of life.   I. Marie, Danielle 1948-
BJ1581.2.S756   1992
170'.44—dc20

Printed in the United States of America on acid-free paper
10 9 8 7 6 5 4 3 2 1

Interior and cover design by Michele Lanci-Altomare
Edited by Gina Renée Gross

A portion of the author's royalties will go to charity.

With love I dedicate this book to
Crystal Barile,
Linda Bowhall,
Carol Loy,
and Linda Taylor—
four perfect friends!

ACKNOWLEDGMENTS
♥

**With love and appreciation,
I would like to acknowledge the following people,
for they have truly made a difference in my life:**

Betty Helbling, my mother, who taught me what giving is all about; Mathilda Helbling, my grandmother, a special woman who lives a life of love; Todd Berreth, my son, a very special and loving person who is a wonderful gift to this world; Robert Leathers, my publisher, who is living his dream of making a difference in the world; Diane Fallon, Allwon's managing publisher, an extremely talented woman who knows how to make work fun; Gina Renée Gross, my editor, who with great skill masterfully put all the words together; Michele Lanci-Altomare, the book's designer, for her magnificent cover and interior design; Dominick Abel, my agent, for his expert guidance; my loving friends, Joanne Bishop, Victoria McMahon, and Colby Smith, who supported my efforts throughout the project; and all the assistants, agents, publicists, business managers, friends, and all the wonderful people I have met who helped me contact all the people in this book, a special thank you.

♥

A WORD FROM THE PUBLISHER

♥

Imagine, if you will, a shell on the beach, spiral in shape. It rests alone on its mound of sand, while behind it the great blue ocean from which it came rolls in and out from shore. And nearby, on other mounds, are other shells, also alone. They cover the gritty landscape as far as the eye can see. At first glance, these shells may look like litter, like identical products of an oceanic assembly line: hard body, sloping shape, ivory color. But if you look more closely, each one yields its subtle uniqueness. This one mottles into pink down toward the back; that one's whorls are like chambers of the ear. Once you have looked, there is no more "litter." There is only a universe: unique, connected, utterly sacred. And, though unique unto yourself, you are one with it.

In our fast-paced, technological world, when so many problems have been pushed to their extremes, it is easy to think that the problems are too big and overwhelming for any individual to have an effect. Each person asks bewilderedly, "How can I make a difference?"

Happily, many of us are asking this question. In *Straight from the Heart,* seventy-five people from the fields of entertainment, psychology, business, spiritual leadership, politics, economics, the arts, and healing share their best findings. What they have found depends upon where they have looked. Some counsel us to look within. Others look to change society. Some advocate thinking globally and acting locally. Some writers counsel positive thinking, others counsel the acceptance of grief. And some see our service to humanity as our service to God. Enjoy, then, the sampling of solutions. Despite their different approaches, all seventy-five writers agree that you *can* make a difference. As actor Jimmy Hawkins says, "Each person's life touches so many other people's lives that if they weren't around, there would be an awful hole."

♥

ANGELES ARRIEN

♥

". . . the arms of love are gratitude, validation, recognition, appreciation, and acknowledgment. When we open ourselves to the arms of love and truly receive love, we experience peace."

The title of the old song "Love Is a Many Splendored Thing" is a reminder that when we remember our splendor and express who we truly are, joyously, the result is peace.

Many indigenous cultures hold the belief that the heart is four-chambered; full-hearted, open-hearted, clear-hearted and strong-hearted. When we are half-hearted rather than full-hearted, we lack the sense of peace. When we are close-hearted rather than open-hearted, we lack the experience of peace. When we experience the doubting heart rather than the clear, trusting heart, we experience confusion and the lack of peace. When we are weak-hearted (lacking the courage to be who we are) rather than strong-hearted, we lack the experience of peace.

In many ways love and peace are inseparable Siamese twins. Where there is peace there is love and where there is love, as expressed by the four-chambered heart, there is peace.

Cross-culturally, the arms of love are gratitude, validation, recognition, appreciation, and acknowledgment. When we open ourselves to the arms of love and truly receive love, we experience peace. One person can make a difference by modeling love in both family and professional contexts. It is contagious.

Angeles Arrien, Ph.D, is a cultural anthropologist, educator, and author and founder of the Four-Fold Way Program. Her teachings are based on the universality of values, ethics, and experiences as they relate to myths, symbols, and the arts. The author of *The Tarot Handbook: Practical Applications of Ancient Visual Symbols* and the forthcoming *The Four-Fold Way: The Paths of Warrior, Teacher, Healer, and Visionary* and *Signs of Life: The Five Universal Shapes and How to Use Them,* Arrien honors her Basque heritage by lecturing nationally and internationally in cross-cultural anthropology and transpersonal psychology at colleges, universities, corporate settings, and growth centers.

NATHANIEL BRANDEN

♥

To the extent that an individual chooses to live consciously, responsibly, and with integrity, he or she produces the result we call self-esteem. Self-esteem is the foundation for treating others with respect and benevolence. And therefore, it is the starting point for transforming the world. If, further, one genuinely wishes to help bring peace to the world, no issue is more vital than to oppose by every means available the notion that it can be for some individual—or some group (including the government)—to impose its ideas on others by the use of physical force. Until individuals and governments renounce the *initiation* of physical force, as a means to settle disputes or impose "ideals," a peaceful world will be impossible. I stress the word "initiation" because every society recognizes the right to use force in self-defense (unless, of course, the offender is the state, in which case self-defense is legally forbidden). This commitment to non-coercion means and entails not only freedom of speech and thought, but freedom of production and trade among consenting adults.

D r. Nathaniel Branden, Ph.D., distinguished psychologist, psychotherapist, and director of the Branden Institute for Self-Esteem in Beverly Hills, is recognized internationally as "the father of the self-esteem movement." He is the author of many books on self-esteem, including the national best-sellers *The Psychology of Self-Esteem, Honoring the Self,* and *How to Raise Your Self-Esteem.* He is in private practice in Los Angeles, where he offers self-esteem seminars and works as a consultant to businesses and other organizations.

KEN KEYES

♥

We humans are too diverse to be able to like everything people do or say. However, to make our own lives work best, we need to learn to love everyone unconditionally, including ourselves. We can always love the human being, even if we don't like what he or she does or says. This is the cutting edge of psychological and spiritual growth: to be able to genuinely and unconditionally appreciate and love a person and simultaneously be able to like or dislike that person's actions and respond with wisdom. This skill enables us to perceive clearly and keep our hearts open. It is the key that opens the door to happiness.

—♥—

Ken Keyes, Jr., author of seven best-selling books, including *Handbook to Higher Consciousness, The Power of Unconditional Love, How to Enjoy Your Life in Spite of It All,* and *Discovering the Secrets of Happiness,* is the founder of the Science of Happiness. Thousands of people from coast to coast have taken his workshops to learn how to apply these effective techniques to their everyday lives. He is the founder of the Ken Keyes Center in Coos Bay, Oregon, that offers courses for people who want to increase their enjoyment of life.

GERALD JAMPOLSKY

"People are beginning to question the values that have imprisoned humankind for many centuries."

I am convinced that our true state of mind is wholeness, containing only the purity of love. In that state, our minds are joined collectively as one, and we feel forever loved, forever loving, and forever pure. When we isolate ourselves from love and from God, we begin to think of ourselves as independent of God and the world around us, separate and alone. That separated part of the mind is the ego, filled with thoughts based on fear and guilt, leaving very little room for love.

I have spent much of my life obeying the voice of my ego, keeping the presence of love, the voice of love, hidden from my awareness. My attachment to guilt simply smothered that awareness. Guilt and fear are so intertwined that they cannot be separated. Love and guilt cannot exist simultaneously any more than love and fear can.

When I listen to my ego's voice of fear and guilt, it sounds like this: "You don't know what you're doing or how to make decisions. Every time you make a decision, it's the wrong one. You've failed many times before and will go on failing.

Besides, you should be ashamed of yourself for the awful things you did in the past. You are a rotten person. You deserve to suffer and be punished. Go ahead, attack and hurt yourself again. Admit that you're lost in life. You've made a mess of things, and there's no way you can get out of this mountain of garbage you created. You cannot get anywhere from here."

There is not much chance to hear the voice of love when thoughts like those come in like lightning and thunder deafening you to any other voice in your mind. And, as if that is not enough, my ego paints the picture that I am a victim of the world I see, and that the cause of all my problems is outside me. My ego does not want me to take responsibility for anything; it wants me always to blame other people.

The signposts marked out in the road map of my ego are worry, doubt, uncertainty, conflict, and self-righteous anger.

The map of the ego is based on "getting," and it leads us to further illusions. The map of love, on the other hand, is based on "giving," and it leads us to peace of mind.

Today there is much turmoil in the world. Many people are starving, and the specter of nuclear annihilation continues to haunt the planet. Everywhere we look there are examples that the ego can use to validate its position that the world is a terrible place, with plenty of justification for fear. Yet, as I travel around the world I find evidence of a spiritual renaissance. I hear people saying that there must be another way of looking at the world; there just has to be a better way. People are beginning to question the values that have imprisoned humankind for many centuries.

Perhaps we are discovering, at last, that the road map for peace is an inward one, and there is guidance within our hearts to help us on our journey, telling us how to achieve a state of mind and heart where there is only love and happiness, rather than guilt, fear, and anger.

Millions of men and women have had their lives transformed by Dr. Gerald Jampolsky's pioneering work in the field of attitudinal healing and by his best-selling books *Love Is Letting Go of Fear, Good-bye to Guilt, Teach Only Love,* and *Out of Darkness into the Light*. This noted psychiatrist, formerly on the faculty of the University of California Medical Center in San Francisco, is the founder of the Center for Attitudinal Healing in Tiburon, California. Jampolsky has spoken worldwide before medical and lay audiences and has appeared on many television programs, including "The Phil Donahue Show" and "60 Minutes." His forthcoming book is entitled *Me First and The Gimme Gimmes.*

BRIAN O'LEARY

♥

It is clear that leaders such as Gandhi and Jesus have made an enormous difference. But how about some of the rest of us, who have not been so positioned? I believe scientific evidence is growing that, through positive thinking and opening up to the energy of spirit, we can make a very great difference in creating peace and love around us. Individual healing experiences and mind-over-matter demonstrations such as spoon-bending are just the beginning. Double-blind experiments on the effectiveness of prayer on the well-being of plants and of heart patients conclusively show the benefits of positive intention. Crystals charged with loving energy have been found to influence the chemistry of fruit juices, such that they are preserved significantly longer. Each of us has the opportunity to radiate love through his or her thoughts and actions to create a more peaceful world. Science, at last, is telling us this loudly and clearly!

Brian O'Leary received his Ph.D. in astronomy from the University of California at Berkeley in 1967, and has since published over one hundred peer-reviewed articles in the scientific literature in planetary science and astronautics. He was a NASA scientist-astronaut during the Apollo program and was deputy team leader of the Mariner 10 Venus-Mercury television science team. He is the author of *Mars 1999, Exploring Inner and Outer Space,* and other space books, and lectures worldwide on future opportunities in space exploration.

ED ASNER

♥

To spread peace we must first end ignorance. Knowledge, coupled with wisdom, is our best hope for the future.

Versatile, committed, eloquent, and talented are all adjectives that accurately describe actor and activist Edward Asner. Perhaps best known for his award-winning comedic and dramatic portrayal of journalist Lou Grant on the smash comedy "The Mary Tyler Moore Show," Asner won three Emmys in 1971, 1972, and 1975. He garnered the same award for the same character in 1978 and 1980 on the highly acclaimed dramatic series "Lou Grant"—and added two more Emmys with "Rich Man, Poor Man" and "Roots." Asner's new role is that of a bigoted ex-cop on "The Trials of Rosie O'Neill." Recent projects include Oliver Stone's feature *JFK* and the miniseries "Switched At Birth."

Doug Martin Photography

ROBERT ALLEN

❦

Each person is born into this world with a reservoir of talent and a specific set of opportunities. The purpose of life is to uncover these talents, to express them, and to eliminate the barriers that limit you from expressing your talents. When you are being yourself, expressing who you are and giving the gift or talent that you were born to give, that is how you spread the greatest amount of love and peace in the world. That is your special, unique way of making a difference.

─❦─

Robert Allen first entered real estate when he bought and sold his first piece of property after college graduation. Spurred on by this success, Allen chose real estate investing as his profession and established a multi-million-dollar portfolio before the age of thirty. His secret? His unique "nothing down" techniques which are chronicled in a book by the same title. The author of *Creating Wealth* and *The Challenge,* Allen is founder of Challenge Systems, Inc., in California, which utilizes Allen's "wealth training" as a program for anyone wishing to achieve success.

TERRY COLE-WHITTAKER

♥

Who a person is within is what is projected out into the world. If I want peace then I need to be peaceful within the cells of my body, as well as have peaceful emotions and thoughts. One can only give out what one is, and what one is is created by how one experiences one's self to be. I feel that the best way for me to spread love and peace is by loving myself, loving God, and loving others. No one is worth being upset over and no one is worth judging as bad, especially myself. Each encounter and each situation is an opportunity to choose love or fear. If I choose love and peace then I am emanating that vibration to the world. I am that I am.

―♥―

Minister, author, and self-help leader, Terry Cole-Whittaker's message of enrichment has been chronicled in her best-selling titles, *What You Think of Me Is None of My Business, The Inner Path from Where You Are to Where You Want to Be,* and *How to Have More in a Have-Not World.* At the height of her ministry in La Jolla, California, she preached her message to millions of viewers each week on her syndicated television show. In 1985 she left her ministry to take charge of her own spiritual destiny. Currently she lectures throughout the world and holds self-motivation and personal growth workshops and retreats on her farm in Washington state.

SONDRA RAY

♥

"When you know with certainty that your thoughts produce your result, you'll be careful to choose positive thoughts and remind others to do that which is genuine."

The Course in Miracles says that "to teach is to demonstrate." From your demonstration of peace and love, others will learn. You are always demonstrating and, therefore, any situation is a chance to teach love and peace. One person can, therefore, make a difference anytime, anywhere. The first step is making changes in your own mind so that you become as peaceful as possible, as loving as possible, and as pure as possible. The next step is offering that peace, love, and purity to others and society. Be the minister of God. Who is your ministry? Your ministry is your colleagues at your work place, those people you have as clients, those people you live with, those people in your address book, and all those people you meet in general. You can teach them all love and peace. You can inspire others to choose for themselves the highest spiritual thought possible. You can tell them what has worked in your life to make you more pure. Becoming a natural networker is a gift to the planet. Sharing what's real and good with others increases it within you.

The master Babaji says that the formula for happiness is "love, truth, simplicity, and service to mankind." Dedicating all your work to God as a form of worship makes a big difference for you and everyone. Service to humanity is one's main duty. Make your career as service-oriented as possible and join service projects—or develop them yourself. What really makes a difference is getting as enlightened as possible and spreading enlightenment. When you know with certainty that your thoughts produce your result, you'll be careful to choose positive thoughts and remind others to do that which is genuine.

True enlightenment is "making the decision to listen to The Holy Spirit that puts you into peace and love. If you are experiencing negativity, fear, conflict, anger, misery, suffering, or sickness, then you have chosen incorrectly. Choose again. Go to a higher thought. Developing your higher self and becoming all that you can be makes a difference. Then you can become a warrior for God, a warrior against darkness, and you can do great work.

―❤―

Sex therapist, family sociologist, certified rebirther, and spiritual healer, Sondra Ray is the founder of Loving Relationships Training (LRT) and is the author of eleven books, including *Loving Relationships* and *The Only Diet There Is*. An avid world traveler and returned Peace Corps volunteer, Ray is a teacher, seminar leader, and devoted student of spiritual disciplines. Her works have been translated into numerous editions throughout the world, including German, Dutch, Spanish, French, and Swedish. There are over one million copies of her books in print.

JIMMY HAWKINS

♥

As the youngest family member, Tommy, in Frank Capra's *It's a Wonderful Life*, I've seen and shared stories with people who have been greatly inspired by this movie. The message of the film is: Each person's life touches so many other people's lives that if they weren't around, there would be an awful hole. Many people have been moved by this message and, because of it, have touched and changed other lives for the better. So you see, one man, Frank Capra, in his passion to bring *It's a Wonderful Life* to the screen, touched so many lives. I truly believe one man can make a difference. He did in my life.

———♥———

As a successful actor, Jimmy Hawkins claims eighty motion picture credits and a host of television credits. Besides playing Donna Reed and Jimmy Stewart's son, Tommy, in *It's a Wonderful Life*, Hawkins played Donald Ruggles in "The Charlie Ruggles Show," co-starred as "Tagg Oakley" in "The Annie Oakley" series, and played Shelley Fabares' boyfriend on "The Donna Reed Show." He was seen regularly on "Ozzie and

Harriet" and "Petticoat Junction," and co-starred as Elvis Presley's sidekick in the musicals *Girl Happy* and *Spinout*. Hawkins is the coauthor of *It's a Wonderful Life Trivia Book*.

CHARLES T. JONES

♥

"One of the most tremendous blessings of my life resulted from my doing something natural and good for my son which resulted in thousands of parents' children experiencing my happiness."

Abraham Lincoln said, "All I am I owe to my dear mother." Mrs. Lincoln had no idea that she was preparing her son to someday save his country. She did what was natural and good and the world knows the rest.

And so it is with all who live to give. One of the most tremendous blessings of my life resulted from my doing something natural and good for my son which resulted in thousands of parents' children experiencing my happiness. Their happiness continues to multiply my own. This is how I made a difference in the world, and I hope my son continues the tradition.

When my son Jere was fourteen years old he needed a shot in the arm. Through friends giving me books my whole life, I took on new dimensions, and I felt books could do the same for my son. I decided on a strategy that I was sure would get his attention. I knew he was looking forward to that sixteenth birthday when he would be *driving*. I made him a proposition. For every book he read and gave me a report on, I would put ten dollars in a car fund. The idea was "if you read in style, you drive in style; if you read like a bum, you drive like a bum."

Overnight he developed a tremendous interest in books. The first book he read was *How to Win Friends and Influence People*. I picked the books and they were all biographies, or self-improvement or religious titles. He read twenty-two books. Did he buy a car? No! He kept the money and used my car and my gas. Did the project succeed? Yes! Far beyond anything I could have imagined. When he went off to college, he began writing me a postcard every day. Many cards brought tears to my eyes because I could tell you the books where his thoughts came from. I expected the cards to cease the second year but they came right through his senior year. I should add that these were among the most difficult years of my life and he can never know the lift his thoughts on the cards gave me.

I began telling this experience in my seminars and read a few cards. I began receiving letters asking for the list of books that I used. One day I received a letter from a grandfather who thanked me for the idea. He said his record was seven grandchildren, six years, twenty-seven thousand pages, and three hundred books. He paid them a penny a page and enclosed the legal contract that he negotiated with each grandchild. I have sent thousands of these to all who request them.

Charles "Tremendous" Jones is internationally known as a salesman, executive, motivator, author, lecturer, and humorist. He entered the life insurance field at age twenty-two and received his agency's Most Valuable Associate award at twenty-three. Ten years later he had received every management honor for sales recruiting and management. At age thirty-seven his agency topped $1 million in force, after which he retired to devote his efforts to lecturing, writing, and consulting activities. Jones's book *Life Is Tremendous* has over one million copies in print and he has addressed more than ten thousand audiences in North America, Australia, and Asia.

DANIELLE KENNEDY

♥

Never take your life or your God-given talents for granted. I've taught my eight children to follow their passions, their talents, and their dreams to the end of the earth. If we follow the signs in our basic personalities and natures that give us clues about ourselves, how can we be miserable? Walk the talk. There are too many big talkers in this world. They make judgement calls and spread conflict. People need to realize this journey on earth should be a mission about personal transformation. If we all started pointing the finger towards our own hearts instead of at those around us, peace would become imminent in our world.

―♥―

Danielle Kennedy sold more real estate in ten years than most do in a lifetime. At the age of twenty-seven, this mother of four with her fifth child on the way decided it was time to start her first career—in real estate. With her time divided between sales calls and the kitchen sink, Kennedy self-corrected with each new prospect, evolving into one of the top agents in the United States for a ten-year period. In her fourth year she had reached 105 closings per year and sustained that record until she became a leading sales trainer, author, and lecturer. Her books, *Super Natural Selling* and *How to List and Sell Real Estate in the 90s,* chronicle her amazing sales techniques and formula for success.

ED McMAHON

♥

I believe there is no better prescription for peace than living by the golden rule. If we really did treat others as we want to be treated, with respect and kindness at all times, we would live in a continually peaceful world.

Between his nighttime television network appearances on "The Tonight Show" starring Johnny Carson, his numerous performances as host on specials and telethons, and his activities in television and radio commercials, Ed McMahon is more familiar to most Americans than their own next-door neighbor. McMahon hosts the syndicated show "Star Search," and cohosts with Dick Clark "TV's Bloopers and Practical Jokes." The spokesman for several major corporations, McMahon has authored two books, *The Art of Public Speaking* and *Superselling*.

ROBERT A. SCHULLER

"The basis for true Christianity is found in a simple but profound statement: God loves you and so do I."

As an ordained minister in the Reformed Church in America, I have spent my life studying the effects the Christian faith has upon the way people live, think, feel, and act. I have determined that the philosophies of the Christian faith are almost as broad as its membership. Therefore, let me first clarify what I consider to be true Christian philosophy and then explain how that philosophy creates the positive characteristics of life to make a difference in your world.

The basis for true Christianity is found in a simple but profound statement: God loves you and so do I. There are two subjects in that sentence; the human and the divine. These are also the subjects of true Christianity.

The divine aspect of Christianity is realizing that our God is a loving, caring, giving God. He is not the God of fire and brimstone, judgement and punishment, that some philosophies have pronounced. Here we find a philosophy that brings hope, joy, peace, and success to the lives of people.

Jesus begins by showing us the attitude that makes the difference. The attitude is, "God is blessing me!" He says, "Blessed are you when people insult you, persecute you and falsely say all kinds of evil against you because of me. Rejoice and be glad, because great is your reward in heaven, for in the same way they persecuted the prophets before you" (Matthew 5:11-12). Jesus lets us know that in all things we can find happiness and joy.

Jesus' next step in introducing us to our God of love is to remind us of how God feels about us. He sees us as great people with great potential. "You are the light of the world, you are the salt of the earth," said Jesus. He goes on to explain that our loving God gave us guidelines for living in order that we might be all that we can be. If we follow these guidelines our lives will soar with wings like eagles.

The guidelines of Jesus Christ can be summed up in one powerful phrase: Love one another. Why is it that people have such a difficult time with this challenge from Christ and with following these guidelines? The fear of extinction. The survival of the species is the most primal motivation. It is the natural fear that drives humans to build the protective walls they feel will help them survive. The walls come in all different shapes and sizes: isolation, addiction to mind-altering chemicals, like nicotine, alcohol, and drugs, violent behavior, inappropriate sexual behavior, inappropriate emotions, irresponsibility, codependency. The list goes on and on. Realizing that our God loves us and cares for us means we really have nothing to fear but fear itself. Consider the words of Jesus: "If God cares for the birds of the air and the grass of the fields, how much more won't he care for you" (Matthew 6:24-34).

My friend, Gerald Jampolsky, says that there are only two emotions: love and fear. In his book, *Love Is Letting Go of Fear*, we see the message Jesus Christ came to bring. Trusting God removes our fears and allows us to love our fellow man. This is the human side of true Christianity. If God is caring for us we can let down our defenses. The walls we've built to protect us can come down. God is our protection. Knowing that God loves us and cares for us lets us then love others.

As we love others and overcome our fears, we become giving people. We can share what we have. We can share our resources of time, energy, and money. The old self is replaced by the new self. We are born again with a new understanding that God truly loves us and we love others. It is comforting to know "God loves me and I love you."

Robert A. Schuller is the founding pastor of the Rancho Capistrano Community Church and president of the Rancho Capistrano Renewal Center in San Juan Capistrano, California. He sits on the board of the nationally syndicated television program, "The Hour of Power," and is seen weekly on that program delivering a message of faith and hope. He has taken his message to churches and conferences throughout the world, including Australia, Brazil, Canada, China, India, Israel, Russia, South Africa, and the United States. Schuller has seven published books, including: *Getting Through the Going Through Stage, Power to Grow Beyond Yourself, World's Greatest Comebacks, Strength for the Fragile Spirit,* and *Just Because You're On a Roll, Doesn't Mean You're Going Downhill.*

SERGE KAHILI KING

♥

One individual always makes a difference in spreading love and peace in the world. Huna philosophy says that there are no limits, and the pertinent meaning here is that we are all connected to everyone and everything in the universe. Therefore everything one does as an individual affects the whole. All thoughts, words, images, prayers, blessings, and deeds are listened to by all that is. The more positive they are, the greater their influence. One person's loving thought is capable of shifting a storm away from a village thousands of miles away. The problem is not that we have influence as individuals, but trusting that we do.

—♥—

Serge Kahili King, Ph.D., has been actively engaged in the fields of parapsychology, paraphysics, bioenergetics, and social technology for more than twenty years. His studies have taken him to many parts of the world, including most of North and South America, Europe, and Africa. King has authored many books, including *Imagineering, Kahuna Healing, Mana*

Physics, and *The Pyramid Energy Handbook,* as well as many articles, courses, and lectures in all his fields of endeavor. King directs the activities of the Order of Huna International, and is engaged in research, teaching, counseling, and healing.

JOEY BISHOP

Fight hatred! Love and peace will surely follow.

A multi-talented actor, comedian, and talk show host, Joey Bishop began his career in burlesque in the late thirties. A charter member of Frank Sinatra's legendary "Rat Pack," Bishop has made a number of feature films, including *The Naked and the Dead*, *A Guide for the Married Man*, *Valley of the Dolls*, *Delta Force*, and *Betsy's Wedding*. Bishop has always been interested in various religions, and is currently cowriting a book with author Marshall Houts entitled *I Believe in God: The Bible Puzzles Me*.

ANNE WILSON SCHAEF

"We need to give up the assumptions, interpretations, and judgements that come from a belief of innate 'rightness' and listen."

ON LISTENING

We have come to a time of listening. So many of us who are writers and celebrities have been so accustomed to "speaking our piece" that we have lost the art of listening. In order really to "listen," we have to *have* time and we have to *take* time.

So often, I hear that native people are "like children" or need to be brought into the Western twentieth century and adopt the ways of Western culture. Yet, my perception is that westerners need to learn from them, to listen to ways that are not understandable to Western culture. We need to give up the assumptions, interpretations, and judgements that come from a belief of innate "rightness" and listen.

We need to listen to the wisdom around us. We need to sit with our elders and "wait upon" their words. We need to sit with our children and feel the wisdom of our ability to be present to their lives. We need to listen to tribal people, not just to absorb their rituals, but to let our souls feel the *wisdom* behind their science, tradition, and rituals.

Then, we will begin to know an old way that is new to us, an unfamiliar that reverberates in the ancient knowing of the soul, a remembrance that bridges with all that is and ever has been—our oneness with all things, people, beings, animals, birds, insects, water, air, stones, plants, and planets. It is only in this knowing that we become who we are and take our place in what we can become.

Anne Wilson Schaef, Ph.D., is an internationally known writer, teacher, facilitator, organizational consultant, philosopher and former psychotherapist. Dr. Schaef is the author of six books, including *Women's Reality, When Society Becomes an Addict, Escape from Intimacy: Untangling the "Love" Addictions,* and *Meditations for Women Who Do Too Much.* Dr. Schaef's specialization in working with the addictive processes, combined with her background as a feminist, has resulted in the development of the concept of Living in Process and Deep Process Facilitation, concepts explored in her forthcoming book, *Beyond Science, Beyond Therapy.* She has been featured on television and radio and has lectured at major conventions, universities, and conferences throughout the world.

DAN MILLMAN

♥

If there is light in the soul, there will be beauty in the person. If there is beauty in the person, there will be harmony in the house. If there is harmony in the house, there will be order in the nation. If there is order in the nation, there will be peace in the world. —*Chinese Proverb*

I'd like to share an incident: Socrates, the old man described in *Way of the Peaceful Warrior* who became my mentor, was walking with me toward Joseph's cafe one day, when I noticed a poster that asked us to Save the Whales. Nearby was another poster with the face of a destitute child and a third poster asked for support for the oppressed people of the world.

> **"Look at this, Soc,"** I pointed to the posters, and confessed, **"Sometimes I feel so guilty, doing all this work on myself when there are so many people in need out there...."**
>
> Socrates kept walking, as if he hadn't heard what I'd said. I was about to repeat myself when, quite suddenly, he stopped, turned to me, and said, **"I'll bet you five dollars you can't slap my face."**

"What? What are you talking about?" I asked. "Didn't you hear what I just said—"

"Ten dollars," he said, upping the ante. "And I'll put one hand behind my back."

Well, I ended up taking his challenge, taking a swing, and ending up lying on the ground in a painful wrist-lock. As Socrates helped me to my feet, he said, "Do you notice that a little leverage can be very effective?"

"Yes," I answered, shaking my wrist.

"It's good that you want to help the world," he said. "But you can only help people if you understand them; and you can only understand them if you first understand yourself. Do what you can, of course, but first develop the clarity and courage to know how to exert the right leverage, at the right place, at the right time."

If peace is going to reign in the world, it seems to me that it has to be founded on the individual. Unless we examine our own motives and contact the love inside, how can we effect lasting change? If wars rage inside us, or within our families, how can peace thrive in the world? This concept is not new, but we need to find new ways to implement it, to bring this truth to life.

Many people offer uplifting words, reminding one another about concepts like "love" and "peace." This, I've noticed, has not been altogether effective, unless the speaker's heart has awakened. Wisdom and good advice abound, even on T-shirts. Think Globally, Act Locally. Live Simply so That Others May Simply Live. I've found that everything, even little things, can make a big difference. Since we are all connected, even a simple action to uplift another person is going to reverberate through the universe.

Normally, when we think of "one person making a difference," we think of heroes like Gandhi, or other spiritual or political leaders. Yet there are few people whose calling and destiny drive them to such visibility. In my own life, I've found that a little bit of something is better than a lot of nothing. So rather than becoming frustrated or disheartened trying to tilt windmills and personally save every suffering soul on the planet, I specialize in "little things" I can do here and now, including writing this statement.

There are big things in the eyes of the world—like your own home and money in the bank—but these are little things in the eyes of spirit. There are little things in the eyes of the world, however, that are very big in the eyes of spirit: Perhaps something as simple as paying the bridge toll for the car behind you, or writing a note of thanks to a waiter or waitress at the restaurant. Or wearing a T-shirt with a heart on it, or asking someone's forgiveness, or giving it. Or doing whatever you do in the name of the One, for the highest good of those around you.

I urge my friends to find their own balance in life between giving and receiving. That balance will naturally be different for each of us. I only urge people to do what they feel good about. One person may give up all personal possessions and dedicate his or her life to working with the poor in Calcutta or Bangladesh. Another may focus on making millions of dollars and living in comfort, and from that foundation, generate foundations and trusts and give fortunes to worthy causes. Who is to judge what is best, or to presume that we must all do the same thing?

Personally, I'm doing my best to establish a solid foundation of peace and love within my family, with my most immediate responsibilities, raising loving, secure children. I also sponsor a child in Kenya, my children have pen pals in other countries, we donate a good and growing portion of our income to causes, people, and organizations that are making a difference. And most important, perhaps, I do what I can in daily life to uplift those around me; with a smile, by speaking from my heart, with praise and gratitude.

Ultimately, these words are only chicken scratchings on the page. But if I could reach out and touch your hand, look into your eyes, you would see yourself in a new light, and know that in spite of appearances, you can make a difference right now. What you do is less important than who you are.

Dan Millman is a past world-champion gymnast, university coach, and college professor whose disillusion with "the usual life" sent him around the world and into the depths of his mind and heart. His training and experiences have generated an approach to life he calls the "way of the peaceful warrior." Dan currently writes, teaches, and enjoys life with his family. His books include *Way of the Peaceful Warrior, The Warrior Athlete, Sacred Journey of the Peaceful Warrior,* and, for children, *The Secret of the Peaceful Warrior.* He recently wrote the script for the feature film *The Peaceful Warrior* and is working on a number of new books.

ROB EICHBERG

♥

"Many of us are afraid to notice how powerful we are because we think that if we are responsible for what happens in the world we are consequently obligated to do something about it."

Each of us, you and I, makes an enormous difference on this planet. It isn't that we must do anything special, for everything we think, feel, do, and say has an impact far greater than most of us are willing or able to understand at any given moment. Many of us are afraid to notice how powerful we are because we think that if we are responsible for what happens in the world we are consequently obligated to do something about it. The simple truth is that we are responsible whether we like it or not, and we are always doing something that has an impact whether we acknowledge it or not.

The more conscious we become the more we can choose the type of impact we are having. The less conscious we allow ourselves to be the more we abdicate choice and create the illusion that we are powerless. This applies to our personal experiences, our relationships, our careers, and every other aspect of our lives. Each individual is responsible for creating love, peace, and harmony in his or her personal life and in the world we live in.

When we harbor hatred and prejudice toward other individuals or groups, these feelings get expressed in many covert and overt ways. When we are fearful we protect ourselves by creating an illusion that we are somehow separate from that which we fear . . . from that which we must guard ourselves against. Defensiveness begets offensiveness. We are creating the language and experience of separation . . . the language and experience upon which disharmony, discord, turmoil, and, ultimately, war is based. When we love ourselves, and put aside our judgements and prejudice, we open the door to loving and accepting others. We begin to notice that we are all one. This awareness is the pathway to love and peace in the world. We begin to treat others as we would want to be treated, to love each other as we want to be loved.

As I began to write this, I thought of the many friends I've lost to AIDS during the past ten years. I believe many of these people would be alive today, and the AIDS epidemic would be over, if we valued human life rather than valuing only some human lives, such as those of people whom we approve of or understand. Until this disease is dealt with as all of ours it will not be eradicated. If we do not learn this lesson more and more people will have to get sick before we put those mechanisms in place to end the epidemic and ultimately create wellness. Health and wellness are based on harmony and love. Harmony and love are both individual and collective experiences. Magic Johnson's 1991 disclosure that he is HIV infected did a great deal to further the consciousness that AIDS is everyone's issue. Yet this disclosure did not change the reality that was always present, it merely brought it to greater consciousness. The most critical message to get across is that we must love one another. In reality we are all one. AIDS is a way of teaching us this.

When my dear friend, television executive Barry Lowen, was dying from AIDS, he received hundreds of letters, yet one in particular had a major impact on Barry. It was from the shoeshine man at Twentieth Century Fox who wanted Barry to know that he had always made him feel important and valuable. The love Barry conveyed with simple dignity on a daily basis came back to him in many forms. Not only did Barry make a lasting difference in Shoeshine's life, but in acknowledging that, Shoeshine made an enormous difference in Barry's life and passing.

You, too, make a difference every day of your life. Take a moment to acknowledge yourself for the gift that you are to others. Take the time to send a note, make a call, or find some other way to simply acknowledge the people in your life who make a difference to you. You can spread love and peace in the world, in your world, simply because who you are really is a radiant energy and all you have to give and receive is love. Let yourself remember!

Rob Eichberg, Ph.D., is a licensed clinical psychologist. He is the author of *Coming Out: An Act of Love,* creator of The Experience, a weekend workshop held throughout the country that concentrates on truth, love, and living powerfully, and co-founder and chair of National Coming Out Day.

MARIANNE ALIREZA

♥

One individual can make a difference in spreading love and peace in the world by making a serious effort to learn about other people and other countries and recognize their differences, not judge them because of these differences. Travel technology and sophisticated telecommunications have brought about an interdependent world where the need to know and understand have become critical needs.

―♥―

Marianne Alireza is the author of *At the Drop of a Veil*, a memoir of the first Christian Western woman to live as a member of one of Saudi Arabia's most prominent families. After her marriage in California, she was whisked to a land thousands of miles away. Veiled like a biblical figure, she lived in a harem for fifteen years until her husband divorced her, depriving her of any right to their five children, according to Moslem law, forcing her to engineer their escapes.

KENNETH BLANCHARD

♥

In *What Color Is Your Parachute?* Richard Bolles talks about people developing their own mission statement. He has a wonderful concept in there about how people can make a difference in the world by making moment-to-moment decisions that add more justice, love, forgiveness, and the like, to the world. I agree wholeheartedly. Find and live your mission.

———♥———

A speaker and business consultant, Kenneth Blanchard, Ph.D., is best known as the creator of the *One Minute Manager* books that have collectively sold more than 7 million copies. Coauthor with Dr. Paul Hersey of the textbook *Management of Organizational Behavior* and *The Power of Ethical Management* with Dr. Norman Vincent Peale, Blanchard is chairman of Blanchard Training and Development, Inc., a full-service management consulting and training company. He also maintains a faculty position at the University of Massachusetts, Amherst, and holds a visiting lectureship at Cornell University.

PAUL COTÉ

♥

"And in his order of things there was reason whereby all things sustained all other things and all things in creation had a role to play in the sustenance of creation itself."

OF LOVE AND PEACE

And in the beginning there existed only the Almighty and he was mightily troubled for he knew not the cause of his own existence. He surmised that some reason for his power must exist and thereupon decided to create a vast emptiness called "space" within which he might exercise his power. Thereafter he conjured up a thing called "matter" and with space as his canvas and matter as his paint, he began the creation.

And as he stood in the center of space he decreed that matter shall be formed in circles that allow a view of all being created and cause very little damage when bumping into that which already had been wrought. And being enamored so of circles he created the stars and planets and moons and set all circles spinning in larger circles around each other in other circles. And when all of this had been wrought he called it the "order" and thereupon the creator was pleased and rested for about 200 million years.

Awakening, he was still troubled for he knew that many things in the creation remained unfulfilled and he decided that there should be living "creatures" in the creation. He thought mightily as to how all of this was to be and he thereupon decided that matter must beget matter, and that one form of matter may take purpose and transform itself into other forms of matter. He then created "life" for all things that grow and oceans and fishes great and small and forests and jungles, and as time went on he made a number of changes in that which he had created and thus he called those changes "evolution." And in his order of things there was reason whereby all things sustained all other things and all things in creation had a role to play in the sustenance of creation itself.

And the Almighty was happy and looked upon the "life" he had created with great satisfaction. Some millions of years later the Almighty again grew troubled for he felt that some part of "life" had been overlooked for nothing in his creation offered joy for all that had been wrought. He then decreed that there should be "music," which would be the only thing in creation that would not be either of matter or made of circles.

But alas, of all things in creation, no creature nor growing thing had that which could offer music. He thereupon laid evolution heavily upon a creature that he had called an "ape"—such that this creature should be able to play "music." Slowly the creature moved from beating twigs upon the trunks of trees to many other more harmonious forms of music, which pleased the Almighty greatly. As was willed, this creature did propagate itself widely and in time music was heard on all parts of the planet earth and throughout other parts of space.

But the Almighty soon became saddened with that which he had wrought because the joy of the music offered by this creature was diminished as the species did not live in accordance with the order of things. It propagated itself to the point where none of the many things that had been created were left, and many things within the seas and upon the lands that the creator hath wrought were devastated. It cared not for its own and defiled all living things. The Almighty then sent many holy and learned men amongst the species to teach the species the meaning of things—this teaching he called "love" and from love came that which he called "peace," which was the form of creation. And while some hope was gained from the teachings, the Almighty remained saddened for love and peace were not abundant and the species continued to tear asunder that which the Almighty hath wrought.

And he observed that of all the creatures, only this species blushed, and knew that it had good reason to do so. And so the Almighty sent another teaching to the species that even the smallest circle of the matter he hath wrought, "the atom," held—the power to destroy the species. The species must, through love, honor and respect the order of things and all that the Almighty hath wrought.

And the Almighty was then weary. He rested again knowing that when he awoke that either the species would have learned to love and live in peace as was his will, or would not have heeded his teachings, in which case all life that the Almighty hath wrought on the planet earth shall be devastated.

Paul Coté is best known as the founder of Greenpeace, a worldwide environmental preservation organization active in seventeen countries. A Canadian citizen and Olympic bronze metalist, Coté is an executive of his land development company. He stays sane by sailing and being married to "a wonderful wife who makes me very happy and quite fat."

RICHARD MOSS

♥

". . . the question of how to spread love and peace grows in part from a perception of people's lack and is rooted in a dynamic of rejection and fear. But it also grows from something else: the impulse toward consciousness."

The idea of making the spread of love and peace in the world into a "how to" is, for me, an oxymoron. Well intentioned as it seems, it is an extraordinary form of the basic egotism that dominates our time and points to a poorly understood, but fundamental riddle.

The minute we want to know "how"—which is really the same as trying to make something conscious—we have separated ourselves from the very dimension of being in which we are already established in love and are, therefore, conducting love moment by moment. We have decided that the spread of love is a worthy task or goal. Therefore we are not at peace. On the contrary, the question of how to spread love and peace grows in part from a perception of people's lack and is rooted in a dynamic of rejection and fear. But it also grows from something else: the impulse toward consciousness.

Nature, itself, is the perfect exemplar of love and peace. Every creature is distinctly itself, has its own incredible subjective expression of beingness, and is in perfect communion with every other creature. Only human beings in becoming conscious fall out of communion with their world. Our dilemma is that as we become conscious of the web of wholeness that is love and the innate oneness and community of nature that is peace, we interrupt the wholeness and become separate from that oneness, thus triggering the desire to spread love and peace. The riddle is that the return to that love is not a "how to" or any other activity or desire born of the perception of a need for love and peace. Nor is it a spiritual "how to" about releasing in faith and surrendering toward a new pattern (that is really very old and ever-present). Those that know this, who really know it in their deepest beings, have passed through (and forever pass through) a fire and are the very founts of love and peace in this world.

Richard Moss, M.D., left the practice of medicine in 1976 and has since led workshops throughout the world. He is widely regarded as an inspirational teacher and master of awakening individuals into new dimensions of consciousness. His work bridges traditional medical, psychological, and spiritual thinking and moves into the direct experience of higher consciousness. Author of *The I That Is We, The Black Butterfly,* and *How Shall I Live,* Moss founded Three Mountain Foundation, an organization that provides workshops, lectures, tapes, and other writings based on Dr. Moss's work.

MARILYN VAN DERBUR

If you can live your dream, you will discover a way to make a difference.

Marilyn Van Derbur is one of the outstanding women in America today. Since being crowned Miss America, Van Derbur has spent the last twenty-five years as a keynote convention speaker. She established an adult survivor program in Denver through the Marilyn Van Derbur Motivational Institute, which focuses on researching the effects of incest and dealing with survivors' abuse. Van Derbur commits her life to trying to stop the sexual violations of children.

BOB HOPE

A comedian has it easy. Just make someone laugh and you've given that person an instant vacation. But anyone can make a difference in the world by giving a little of himself or herself to someone who is less fortunate.

In the entire history of show business, no individual has traveled so far—so often—to entertain so many, as comedian Bob Hope. "The King of Comedy" has starred in sixty movies, holds fifty-three honorary doctorates, has written and published ten books, and has triumphed in all five major show business media—vaudeville, stage, motion pictures, radio, and television. He makes hundreds of personal appearances and benefit shows each year, and many charities profit by his talents: The Parkinson Foundation, Vietnam veterans groups, CHILDHELP USA, Habitat for Humanity, and Hughen Center for the Handicapped Children. Whether entertaining the men and women in Saudi Arabia serving "Operation Desert Storm" or hosting a golf classic that provides over $1 million in contributions for forty desert charities in the Palm Springs area, Hope is truly "Mister Number One."

Cylla Von Tiedemann

JEAN HOUSTON

♥

HUMAN LOVE EXTENDED THROUGH THE BELOVED
In 1975, I helped to organize and chaired a conference at the United Nations at which Mother Theresa of Calcutta was one of the guests. A tiny woman bristling with joyous energy, she seemed so open and available that I found myself asking her:

> "Mother, how does it happen that you are able to do so much, and why are you in this state of joy?"
>
> "My dear," she said, "it is because I am so deeply in love."
>
> "But Mother, you're a nun!"
>
> "Precisely," she said. "I am married to Jesus."
>
> "Yes, I understand, you're married to Jesus. All nuns are."
>
> "No, you don't understand," she countered. "I really am. I am so in a state of love that I see the face of my Beloved in the face of the dying man in the streets of Calcutta. I see my Beloved in the day-old child who's left outside our convent, and in the

leper whose flesh is decaying; and I can't do enough for my Beloved! That is why I try to do something beautiful for God."

What is the nature of the conquest by love? The more deeply we encounter the Divine Beloved, the more sensitively we feel the agony of the world, the more we are called to creative action. In the light of the enhancement of your inner and outer sensibilities, you will necessarily feel more, care more, and think more deeply about the decay in the social and moral order. There is usually a tension between the joy felt in the presence of love and the agony felt in an enhanced awareness of suffering in the world. Finding yourself in union with the Beloved, you also find yourself woven into the fabric of the world; having partnered the depths, you are also extended over the breadth of creation. As long as there is illness, bloodshed, hunger, war, racial tension, discrimination, exploitation, prejudice, poverty, rejection, and disempowerment, you live with an undercurrent of sorrow, regardless of the quality of your joy. Evil and aberration exist in both internal as well as external worlds, and the lover of God has to reach out to allay or redeem the suffering of both. Together with the Beloved, you reach out to do what you can in the light of the perspective of grace and the energy of spiritual partnership.

Every human being has a unique destiny, an entelechy; and in communion with the Beloved, you begin to have a profound respect and even awe for the other person's godded potential. Certainly one of the primary exemplars of this attitude was Jesus, who could say and do remarkable things for others and be in reverence before them. The Christos is always the "you" who is in reverence before the entelechy or godseed in the other. In the mystery of love, as you learn to love another truly, you find the Divine Lover revealed within that other human being. That Divine Lover mirrors your Beloved and is, in some sense, the same. Then, like Mother Theresa, you cannot do enough for the other, for you cannot do enough for the Beloved. You are looking at the other with the eyes of the Beloved when you are able to see him or her in wonder and astonishment, in the fullness of human glory, even amid the conditions of everyday life. This "double vision" empowers and releases the other to become who or what he or she truly is. This is the "look of love."

The esoteric commandment implied by the great commandment to love is that you must become a mediator of love to all you meet. Contact with the Beloved of the soul allows you to become midwife of the possibilities, both human and divine, in others. In this role you render yourself diaphanous to the Beloved of both yourself and the other and try to be a genuinely humble example and instrument of the grace of love you have experienced in encountering the Divine Beloved. In this ministry of love you are always servant and never lord.

Dr. Jean Houston is an internationally acclaimed author, teacher, and leader in the science of human development. Her work blends myth, history, philosophy, and psychology with music, meditations, movement, and dance to help realize latent human potentials. Past president of the Association of Humanistic Psychology, she is director of the Foundation for Mind Research in Pamona, New York, and is author of eleven books, including *The Possible Human, Search for the Beloved, Mind Games,* and *Listening to the Body.*

LEIGH STEINBERG

♥

"I attempt to reach out and truly touch something in someone on a deeper human level when I negotiate with that person. If I can touch that person's heart, then that is truly what making a difference is all about."

I believe that one person can make an incredible difference in the world, and I realize the impact that athletes can make on society—with the right mentorship.

Anyone who is going to be associated with our organization must start with an understanding of the values of self-respect, family, and community. We want our athletes to have, or be able to develop, a holistic sense where they perceive themselves as human beings first, have a well-defined social conscience, and understand the importance of being role models.

I don't think the negotiating I do contributes an enormous amount to life, but the one-on-one relationships with the athletes and helping them develop strong values do. Also, being able to go across the country and establish charitable community foundations, and *really see* a difference being made, is just fantastic.

There is a critical difference between problem solving and confrontation negotiating. I attempt to reach out and truly touch something in someone on a deeper human level when I negotiate with that person. If I can touch that person's heart, then that is truly what making a difference is all about.

As the United States' leading sports attorney, Leigh Steinberg has represented the first player selected in the last three national football league (NFL) drafts—Troy Aikman, Jeff George, and Russell Maryland. In 1991, Steinberg set several records in his career as a sports agent; he not only represented the first NFL draft pick but also the selected second, Eric Turner, as well as Seattle Seahawks' Dan McGwire. With a client list that reads like a "Who's Who" of professional sports, including such stars as Warren Moon, Jeff George, Greg Anthony, and Steve Young, Steinberg's desire is to lessen the spotlight on the "big bucks" mentality of professional sports and make the players realize their potential to influence people and act as positive role models in today's society.

BERNARD GUNTHER

♥

peace

yourself
together

———♥———

Bernard Gunther, Ph.D., was for thirteen years a pioneer at the Esalen Institute where he created the Esalen Massage. He is the author of many best-selling books including, *Energy Ecstasy, Sense Relaxation, What to Do Till the Messiah Comes, How the West Is One,* and *The One Minute Enlightenment.* Dr. Gunther is currently working in Los Angeles with his own unique method for the practical application of enlightenment and mind-body-spiritual integration.

RICK DEES

♥

"When you take the time to care about others and help them along their paths, they feel great, you feel great, and the world is just a little bit brighter."

This is not something I would usually ever talk about. But if someone else can benefit as I have, then I am happy to pass along what are probably my three most important guiding principles.

First, approach everything with the spirit of giving. This goes for both private and professional life. Without making a big noise about it, if you can help someone out, if you can intervene to just give that person a chance, do it. Help in whatever way is needed. Try to make a difference directly in people's lives. Sometimes the opportunity comes one-on-one, sometimes on a larger scale through an organization. Just grab every opportunity. When you take the time to care about others and help them along their paths, they feel great, you feel great, and the world is just a little bit brighter.

Next, try to concentrate on doing only the things of which you can feel proud. Why contribute to all the negativity? There is already plenty of that in the world and in people's lives. Before you go ahead, consider how something you are going to do will affect people. Will it make them feel happy and good about themselves?

Finally, when you say you're going to do something, do it. It is easy to go off in all directions with plans, but the key is to actually come through for people, to complete what you say you will do. You have got to finish what you set out to do.

———♥———

Since 1982, Rick Dees has been a top radio personality in America. His "Rick Dees Weekly Top Forty" is heard on over 350 radio stations across the United States; his "American Music Magazine" goes around the world and on the Armed Forces Network; and he remains a dominant airwaves presence in Southern California. Dees's charitable activities have included the March of Dimes, Big Brothers, and Spare Change, a group that focus on the homeless. In 1986, he formed Broadcasters Against Drugs (BAD), an organization that has enjoyed wide national success discouraging any on-air glamorization of drug and alcohol use.

JACK CANFIELD

♥

". . . I realized that the source of all love started with self-love and self-acceptance. I believe peace between people and peace among nations starts with peace within one's self."

I believe one person can make a huge difference in spreading love and peace in the world. It is simply a matter of intention and choice. When I made love a focus in my life, and constantly put attention on spreading it, it began to continually unfold in my life.

I made a conscious choice to devote my life to bringing more love and peace to the world when I was twenty-nine years old. At about the same time I realized that the source of all love started with self-love and self-acceptance. I believe peace between people and peace among nations starts with peace within one's self. So I began to devote my life to learning and teaching as much as I could about self-acceptance, self-love, and self-esteem.

When I first began, I attended thirty-eight weekend workshops in one year on every conceivable aspect of self-development and spiritual growth. Out of that experience I formulated a model of holistic development that I began to teach to parents, teachers, administrators, counselors, managers, and the general public. Since then, I have written four books, three curriculum guides, eight audio albums (including one translated into Spanish), video programs, and hundreds of trainings. I share the message everywhere, and in every way I can. I also train thousands of teachers a year and every summer we train seventy new facilitators, thus attempting to multiply myself and my message as much as possible.

But most importantly, I try to live the message. I try to be a model of love and peace in my life. I meditate and pray as much as possible. I do exercises to develop my patience and my compassion. I tune into the source of all love and grace to constantly reconnect myself to the spirit within. Then I follow my intuition, and trust my heart. When I get off center too much, I see a therapist to heal my childhood wounds.

I attempt to see all experiences as grist for the mill—opportunities for expanding my capacity to love and relate. I believe in the findings of Raymond Moody reported in his book *Life After Life*, in which he states that the purpose of life is to expand our capacity to love and to expand our level of wisdom. I remind myself that that's the earth's curriculum. That is our life's purpose.

I believe that when I live my life from this context, then everything I do contributes more love and peace in the world. My main work focus is in helping individuals heal and develop in the area of self-love. This I believe spills over into their outer relationships, and finally into the organizations (political, economic, social) that they live and work with. Some days I feel like I make a big difference and other days my contribution feels small, but I have seen over and over again that it all adds up. There is a cumulative effect. Every day there are more and more conscious people moving into positions of influence in the world.

I look at the progressiveness of countries like Germany, the Soviet Union, and South Africa, organizations like Greenpeace, The Tree People, the Twelve Steps and other recovery programs, and so much more that has happened these past years, and I see a tremendous outer reflection of all the inner work that is being done. Everything we do makes a difference and the speed of transformation is accelerating at an ever more rapid pace.

Jack Canfield is president of Self-Esteem Seminars and The Foundation for Self-Esteem in Culver City, California. He is the coauthor of *Self-Esteem in the Classroom* and the forthcoming *Chicken Soup for the Soul*. He has developed self-esteem development programs that are currently operating in some diverse environments, such as New England Telephone Company, the Los Angeles public schools, and San Quentin Prison.

SUSAN STAFFORD

♥

As I make my way through the tunnel of life, there are times when it feels like a never-ending struggle, but my faith continues to renew and the light near the end grows brighter and brighter. I only hope that through my work I can leave a few crumbs along the way that might nourish others. Ultimately I know each of us has to find his or her own way, and therein lies the challenge and the joy of living life. The secret of life is to truly live it. The solution is finding the agape love that was spoken about when He walked two thousand years ago.

Susan Stafford, Ph.D., succeeded in being the first hostess nominated for an Emmy on the game show, "Wheel of Fortune." Her departure from the show after seven and a half years was for a calling to do more with her life, which she achieved through developing documentaries on leprosy, working with cancer and AIDS patients, and earning a Ph.D. in psychology. All of these experiences have culminated in Dr. Stafford currently teaching seminars on stress, coproducing and hosting a pilot called "Secrets and Solutions," and forming her own production company entitled Destiny's Beyond Today Production Company. She is known as the Goodwill Ambassador to the World.

LOUISE L. HAY

♥

I am well known for my advocacy of the use of affirmations in our daily lives. I think that the metaphor I use to describe the power of affirmations might also describe how one individual can make a difference in spreading love and peace in the world.

Think of when it rains. One drop does not seem like much, in fact it may seem like nothing at all. But then comes another drop and then another. Pretty soon you have a rainstorm and from that rainstorm comes a great collective power which contributes to the strength of streams and rivers.

Just think what would happen if each one of those drops thought that it couldn't possibly make a difference and instead went home and stayed in bed. It would be a very dry world. *One* does make a big difference, because it seldom stays "just one," but usually becomes "one plus one plus one. . . ."

I have always believed that in order for you to make a loving difference in the world, you must first learn to love yourself. Not tomorrow, but right now. It is only when you have come to accept everything about yourself that you can begin to affect a change on the outside. Therefore, I lovingly offer you my ten steps to loving yourself:

1. Stop all criticism. Criticism never changes a thing. Refuse to criticize yourself. Accept yourself exactly as you are. Everybody changes. When you criticize yourself, your changes are negative. When you approve of yourself, your changes are positive.

2. Don't scare yourself. Stop terrorizing yourself with your thoughts. It's a dreadful way to live. Find a mental image that gives you pleasure (mine is yellow roses), and immediately switch your scary thought to a pleasure thought.

3. Be gentle and kind and patient. Be gentle with yourself. Be kind to yourself. Be patient with yourself as you learn the new ways of thinking. Treat yourself as you would someone you really love.

4. Be kind to your mind. Self-hatred is only hating your own thoughts. Don't hate yourself for having the thoughts. Gently change your thoughts.

5. Praise yourself. Criticism breaks down the inner spirit. Praise builds it up. Praise yourself as much as you can. Tell yourself how well you are doing with every little thing.

6. Support yourself. Find ways to support yourself. Reach out to friends and allow them to help you. It is being strong to ask for help when you need it.

7. Be loving toward your negatives. Acknowledge that you created them to fulfill certain needs. Now you are finding new, positive ways to fulfill those needs. So lovingly release the old negative patterns.

8. Take care of your body. Learn about nutrition. What kind of fuel does your body need to have optimum energy and vitality? Learn about exercise. What kind of exercise can you enjoy? Cherish and revere the temple you live in.

9. Do mirror work. Look into your eyes often. Express this growing sense of love you have for yourself. Forgive yourself as you look into the

mirror. Talk to your parents as you look into the mirror. Forgive them, too. At least once a day say, "I love you, I really love you!"

10. Love yourself . . . do it now. Don't wait until you get well, or lose the weight, or get the new job, or the new relationship. Begin now—and do the best you can.

Louise L. Hay, D.D., is an author, lecturer, and metaphysical teacher, and *loving the self* is the basis for her work with people. Through her techniques and philosophy, many have learned how to create more of what they want in their lives, including more wellness in their bodies, minds, and spirits. An ordained minister with the Church of Religious Science, Hay is the author of many best-selling books published under her imprint, Hay House, including *Heal Your Body, You Can Heal Your Life,* and *The Power Is Within You.*

ROBIN LEACH

♥

After interviewing hundreds of rich and famous people, it's clear to me that money and fame don't make people happy. You can't buy happiness, love, or peace. It has to come from within. I'd rather have a million smiles in my heart than a million dollars in my pocket! Also, I really believe that anything is possible. Don't think of the obstacles in trying to spread peace and love in the world, *just do it!*

Robin Leach is executive producer, host, and managing editor of the television show "Lifestyles of The Rich and Famous," now in its ninth successful year. He also produces and hosts "Runaway with The Rich and Famous" and the annual special "The Rich and Famous World's Best." Leach is supervising executive producer and host of the forthcoming television special, "Home Videos of the Stars," which is currently being developed as a weekly, half-hour series.

KOREY DHEMING

"We are able to spread more love and peace in the world by being willing to grow, by examining the things about ourselves that are preventing us from being able to love and be loved."

I sat in synagogue one Friday night as my friend got up to speak. When he arrived at the podium, I could feel the tension in the room. The faces around me stared at him in stone cold silence. He smiled warmly at the audience. People did not smile back. He was an Arab. He was going to speak to a room full of Jews about his perspective on relations in the Middle East.

    He told them how he had fought against Israel as a captain in the Egyptian army. He told them how he had been taught to hate the Jews since childhood. Then he told them how, one day, he had decided to step out of himself and try to see the Jewish perspective. He said he became keenly aware that the fear, the mistrust, and the pain that the Arabs were feeling were also felt by the Jews. These negative feelings fed into each other. They were like two mirrors facing each other. One reflected back to the other exactly what the other presented.

My friend, that day, decided to change what his mirror conveyed. He decided that someone needed to give first. Someone needed to look inside and challenge and change what was preventing him from having love and peace in his life. Perhaps then, and only then, would that also change what the other reflected.

He began to open up and be willing to listen. He began to have empathy for the other's perspective. He began to look at the other as wanting just what he wanted—love, peace, happiness, and acceptance. Sure enough, for the most part, his plan began to work. He made some very close friendships with some Israelis and when he came to the United States, he did the same with many Jews here.

That night at my temple, he was so sincere and warm as he spoke. People listened to him. They relaxed. They smiled. The room began to glow. At the end of the service, people surrounded him to greet him, to welcome him, and to ask questions about his culture that they had never been able to ask before. They thanked him and told him he was welcome to return any time. As he was leaving, a woman ran over to his wife, hugged her, and gave her a loaf of challah bread to take home to her family.

Individuals can make a difference in spreading love and peace in the world when they make it their responsibility to do so. This means we all have to try to understand other people's pain even if we don't seem to understand it. It means giving of ourselves rather than waiting for someone else to "do it first." It means not blaming others for our problems, but instead looking inside and seeing what needs changing in ourselves, and then taking action to create those changes. We are able to spread more love and peace in the world by being willing to grow, by examining the things about ourselves that are preventing us from being able to love and be loved. We can commit ourselves to being the best people we can be, regardless of what other people are or are not doing.

Sometimes, even if we reflect love, we may not get it back. This is fine. We must take the risk. For only when a person extends a hand can we be assured that someone, somewhere, will take it. If a person always keeps it in his or her own pocket, that person makes it very difficult for anyone to grasp it.

Imagine how it would be if we all would reach out to each other. Imagine how it would feel if each person would take responsibility for himself or herself, his or her beliefs and part in problems. Imagine what the world would look like if everyone could see that people are all mirrors that reflect to others exactly what is inside of them. It would be wonderful if everyone did all of these things. However, I, as an individual, can't change others. I can't make them see it my way. I can't force them to take the initiative. But I can take the initiative and be the first to reach out. I can challenge my fears and beliefs. I can work to change myself. Peace and love truly do begin with me.

Korey Levin Dheming, M.S.W., is a teacher, writer, and therapist. She owns and operates a tutoring business in Pacific Palisades, California, where she teaches teenagers how to get good grades in school, how to feel good about who they are, and how to take responsibility for themselves. She is also the author of the forthcoming book: *Becoming an "A" Student: Study Skills for Teenagers and Their Parents.*

BOYD WILLIT

♥

It is the nature of a human's mind to imagine perfection in everything he or she touches. Yet perfection lives only in the domain of the gods. It is the person's job to discover that line where mortal stops and celestial begins. We are to be inspired by the gods and their perfection, inspired, but not made to become one.

Boyd Willit is a father, husband, businessman, designer, inventor, and shaman. This unique combination of abilities has led him into careers as diverse as his current role: co-owner of a multi-million-dollar company called Harper House that distributes stationery and gift products of Willit's design. Harper House's main specialty is the popular "Day Runner," a three-ring color binder that is essentially a desk in the form of a book.

PAT ALLEN

MY SPIRITUAL LAWS

These spiritual laws came to me in a dream in 1984. The experience was strange; I could open my eyes, turn on the light, copy the words down, fall asleep, and forget the whole experience. It was not until 1987 that I was asked by a Science of the Mind church to present a sermon. I did, and my life changed. As I spoke about what these ideas meant to me, I realized that they were my spiritual laws and I had better live by them. The audience responded to my laws, and obviously they needed to hear them. Copies of these laws have been printed and handed out and they seemingly make a difference in the lives of those who have read them. I feel humbled by the gift of these awarenesses. They feel a little "miraculous" for my scientific mind, yet it was my experience, and I have benefitted immensely from them.

1. Live to love God through service to mankind.

2. Study the spiritual path daily before rising.

3. Discipline the body in order to free it, to enjoy its senses fully.

4. Be grateful for daily bread in whatever form.

5. Enjoy the fruits of my labor to demonstrate spiritual abundance on earth for others to emulate.

6. Avoid people who are "vexations" to the spiritual path, for they invite self-destruction through frustrations and resentments.

7. Pursue being a woman with a career of some size, national or local, not a career woman.

8. Serve as a medium for men and women to reach God.

9. Marry the man who best evolves through my medium for he is my spiritual soul mate.

10. Beware of "defiance" on any level—physical, mental, emotional, or spiritual—it will always destroy the spiritual path.

Pat Allen, Ph.D., creator of Semantic Realignment (Want Training), a system for teaching people to get what they want out of life by reversing negative language patterns, and founder of "The Want Institute," is a psychotherapist with fifteen years counseling experience. A rare blend of psychotherapist-counselor-teacher, Allen conducts weekly seminars in Southern California, is author of the book, *Conversational Rape,* and is also a frequent radio and television talk show guest. She has worked with Jane Fonda, Dr. Joyce Brothers, Phyllis Diller, and Dr. Tony Grant.

RITA DAVENPORT

♥

". . . I learned never to part company, sign a letter, note or autograph, or hang up the phone, without saying 'love you.'"

If each of us would open up and share just a little of all of the love that he or she has to offer, it would go a long way in helping to spread love and peace in the world.

A friend taught me the importance of sharing my love with others. A few years ago we were talking about the death of her husband. She told me that the one thing she regretted the most was that the morning that he died she forgot to tell him that she loved him. After hearing this I learned never to part company, sign a letter, note or autograph, or hang up the phone, without saying "love you." The one thing that you have to remember is that once you start you can never stop because other people will start to say it too. The saying "What goes around, comes around" really is true.

My brother, a big, burly police sergeant, was never a very emotional or sentimental man. But after hearing me say "love you" every time we talked, one day he finally mumbled the words himself. After that, we never ended a conversation without him saying "love you"! People never outgrow the need to hear that they are loved, so if you want to hear it, say it more! "Love you!"

———❤———

Rita Davenport's professional career includes work as a social worker, consumer service specialist, and television producer and broadcaster. Davenport has presented over seven hundred seminars nationwide—to universities, corporations, small businesses, and civic organizations—and has been retained as management consultant to Fortune 500 companies. She has earned national acclaim as an expert in time management and has been featured on "Good Morning America" and "Sally Jessy Raphael." She shared speakers' platforms with Erma Bombeck, Art Buchwald, Art Linkletter, Og Mandino, and Dr. Joyce Brothers. Author of the best-seller *Making Time—Making Money,* Davenport broadcasts her nationally syndicated cable television show "Success Strategies" to over 32 million homes across the country.

RICHARD GREENE

♥

". . . extra dimensions of being and performance and answers to all of our present life problems lie waiting for us, just outside of the box of our self-created limitations."

When I was a child I asked myself two simple questions about life, "Who are we?" and "Why are we here?"

None of the answers I heard moved me. The unwillingness of most adults to even ask these questions confused me and still does. It seems that most humans are trapped so deeply in ruts of a lifestyle they have become prisoners to that they can no longer even imagine the forest, let alone see it from the trees.

It bothered me that our lives on planet earth were based upon the scientific law of cause and effect. "Everything comes from something. Do this and that will happen." But when I would ask an adult where God came from, he or she would shrug and say, "He didn't come from anywhere or anyone. He always was, and always will be." It seemed that there were other dimensions of being that were available to us as human beings to jump into if we wanted to. Why can't we also operate in that infinite space? But no one seemed to be able to make the connection, the bridge between who we really are and who we have all agreed to pretend we are in these physical lives on earth.

This stubborn mind-set was really unacceptable to me. I was, as a kid, and I remain, unwilling to view my life in the artificial box of little "r" reality handed down from past generations. I was, and I remain, unwilling to divorce my life from the magic of the universe. I know that extra dimensions of being and performance and answers to all of our present life problems lie waiting for us, just outside of the box of our self-created limitations.

As I see it, our lives, once described as "parenthesis in eternity," are infinitely more remarkable than we can imagine. Like the baseball player who hits three home runs in one game because he mysteriously sees the ball floating toward him like a grapefruit, a person like Mozart who copies magnificent symphonies out of thin air, or the average person in a state of ecstasy, precognition, or extraordinary creativity who falls into a sort of metaphysical magical state where the normal laws of time and space in the third dimension seem suspended, there is "something more" that is part of our birthright! We are absolutely part of something infinitely larger than balancing our checkbooks, getting to work on time, or decreasing our national debt, no matter how real these issues loom in our daily consciousness. We are an inextricable part of a big "R" reality that holds the big "R" solutions to our lives as individuals and as a species on this planet. Life just doesn't work for us on any level until we accept this larger reality and tap into it.

We make a difference in the world when we challenge others and ourselves to tap into this remarkable space of infinite potential to become who we are underneath this illusion of limitation. We need to bridge our physical reality with a larger spiritual reality. It is this synthesis that is who we really are. In fact, the sound "hu" in spiritual traditions is regarded as "the sound of God." The suffix "man" is the beginning of Latin derivatives for words such as "mano" (hand) or "manifesting." The word "being" is a verb as well as a noun.

So, in the infinite wisdom of the naming of ourselves we actually have the answer to the question of who we are. We are "human beings," that is, "the process of becoming the manifestation (or hand) of the sound of God."

In sports, art, music, drama, and in the simple act of honoring and loving another at work or at home, we humans experience ourselves in transcended states of performance and being where we break through the veil that separates us from other dimensions and literally hook up with an energy inside of ourselves where the third dimensional traps of time and space cease to exist. We make a difference in the world, a real difference, when we remind ourselves to integrate these experiences of spirit or God or essence into our daily lives in every possible way.

Making a difference in our species means raising children in an entirely different way, becoming conscious parents who are aware that every single word, tone, and gesture we use with our young children literally programs their brains and changes their lives. Instead of shaping our children's lives to fit our norms and the expectations of a society that refuses to see the magical dimensions of life as only children can, we make a difference by treating our children as what they truly are—complete, precious seeds from God containing unique, brilliant, and magical parts of the universe. Like beautiful flowers in our garden, we need only to protect them and water them with pure, unconditional love, a very rare quality in today's families.

Other than spreading unconditional love, making a difference is not doing any one thing. Solving business, personal, or planetary problems is not about coming up with a magical, cure-all solution. The challenges for business, for ourselves as human beings, and our species and planet will continue to outstrip specific solutions. By focusing, however, on the multi-dimensional wholeness of who we really are and our individual and species' missions for being here in the first place, we can develop the consciousness and the beingness that will connect us to the spirit and magic in ourselves. That is what you and I are really looking for.

A "reformed attorney" and former radio and television talk show host, Richard Greene now uses his expertise, "the new communication," and neuro-linguistic programming to solve conflicts and create peak performance through his consulting and workshops in fourteen countries around the world. His clients include presidents of countries, political candidates, attorneys, and executives of corporations who want to refine their public speaking impact; businesses and institutions that want to resolve conflicts and increase productivity; Olympic and professional athletes; and parents who want to bring out the fullest potential in their children.

MARK VICTOR HANSEN

♥

"Being on-purpose to do something significant and world-serving puts all the forces of the universe at your service."

One individual with inspiration, aspiration, dedication, and perspiration moving towards a worthwhile and important destination like love and peace makes a significant, impactive, important, beneficial contribution.

Being on-purpose to do something significant and world-serving puts all the forces of the universe at your service. Assuming the goal or objective is big enough, the God factor comes to serve us. We start thinking right, acting right, and commence doing all the right things for the right reasons, getting all the right results right here and right now.

Life has the meaning that we individually and collectively superimpose on it. When we understand the law of polarity that says black/white, concave/convex, in/out, we understand immediately that we are either into creation or, by neglect, into disintegration. People on-purpose for love and peace start by creating it within themselves, then manifesting it externally to themselves. Their powerful energy orbit envelopes those in their energy orbit and stimulates other's thinking. Vision can't be bought or taught it has to be caught. Those of us who deeply understand love and peacefulness from the fully functioning core of our being know that we are creating our reality in the universe and the world with our thinking. Therefore, we see the end of the Middle Eastern conflict as a reason to rejoice, and say we are leaving thoughts of separation and entering thoughts of reconciliation and cooperation; we are ending weaponry and embarking on the path of living fully. We forsake oblivion for utopia. Only now is it possible. Only now can we conceive, believe, and achieve permanent universal love and peace.

Mark Victor Hansen addresses thousands of people annually through corporate programs, national trade and professional associations, and educational and philanthropic institutions around the world. His best-selling book, *Future Diary,* features goal-setting techniques for creating a positive mental attitude. He has been featured in television interviews on ABC, NBC, CBS, and HBO, and has recorded a number of best-selling audio cassette albums.

BETTY BETHARDS

♥

"In working together, we can change the world. We can right all wrongs and correct people's thinking so that we will have a world that works, one where there is love and harmony among the people."

There's no one like you in the whole universe. Each person does count, each person can make a difference. Every person can contribute his or her unique talents, gifts, and abilities like no one else. The world needs each person working to bring out the very best gifts he or she has to share with humankind. In working together, we can change the world. We can right all wrongs and correct people's thinking so that we will have a world that works, one where there is love and harmony among the people.

God is love in all religions. Unless we're living love twenty-four hours a day, we're missing the mark. We have to learn to be loving when it's hard to do—that's the true test of our hearts. In the eyes of God, we're all equal, and if we realize there are truly no race, sex, or class distinctions, there will be no separation between us. We're all connected to the God force. We're all God's children.

The secrets of all time, the secrets of heaven and earth, are locked within you. Each of you has within you a road map that will show you the easiest way to discover these hidden treasures. We all get so distracted in our lives reacting to other people's problems, other people's anger and fears, instead of listening to that inner voice that is within our hearts. You have the power within you to make your life anything you choose. You are getting out of life exactly what you think you deserve—nothing more, nothing less. Your thoughts, words, and actions determine your reality. You can create anything you can dream.

The mind is like a computer. What you program into it becomes your reality. Learn to cancel out your negative thoughts and program in the positive. Clean out the closets of your mind. As you release all the old hurts, guilts, and fears, what you will discover are the talents and gifts that lie within you.

Every situation and experience has a positive lesson for you. They may seem negative at the time, but they are positive opportunities for growth and learning. Everyone you meet and encounter in your life is your teacher, as well as your student. It's important to remember that no one has any power over you unless you choose to give it to them. Set realistic boundaries for the time and attention you can give to that person. Spend time in meditation daily to be sure to recharge your own energy batteries.

Love is the strongest force in the universe. One positive person can change the energy of a thousand negative people. As you align yourselves with this force and go forward, the sky is the limit for what you can create. Visualize and empower your goals. Love yourselves, change what needs changing, and keep what you like. As you begin to love yourself unconditionally *as you are,* you can then learn to love your fellow man or woman in the same way. If you work on yourself and wake up, you'll see all the injustices, all the prejudices in the world, and begin to change them. As we change ourselves, we encourage other people to better themselves.

Learn to be kind to one another and not judge others. It should not be a world of competition, but a world of creativity, where we're happy for one another's successes and truly rejoice in each other's achievements. People tend to put all their anger and fear that's locked up within themselves and dump it on different races, cultures, and religions. People are a mirror for us to see ourselves in. Our problems have nothing to do with people or races "out there"; the anger comes from within us.

This is the most exciting time for humankind. Are we going to wake up and take responsibility for our lives and make this world a better place, or just ignore the situation at hand? I believe as each person sows, he or she will reap. This is why it is so important for everyone to shine their light and contribute whatever gifts, talents, and abilities they have. It matters not how big or small your contribution is, it only matters that you tried to make the world a better place. You can create a world that works!

Betty Bethards is a self-help lecturer, author, mystic, and spiritual healer. The president of the Inner Light Foundation, an entity that provides ongoing programs in the development and understanding of human potential, Bethards has helped millions in their search for self-understanding. Her seminars focus on dreams, meditations, and visualizations and the application of these tools in communication, health, and stress management. The author of *The Dream Book, Be Your Own Guru, Sex and Psychic Energy, Techniques for Health and Wholeness, There Is No Death, Relationships in the New Age of AIDS,* and twenty-nine audio cassettes, Bethard's goal is to teach people to develop and use their own intuitive gifts, talents, and abilities by "helping people to help themselves."

LEE IACOCCA

I'm not sure love and peace get spread. It's more likely that they're just found. And they're usually found when people have a secure home, enough to eat, a future to look forward to, and some dignity in their work. The biggest contribution that most of us can make is to try and see that, for as many people as possible, these things are available.

Lee Iacocca, chairman of the board and chief executive officer of Chrysler Corporation, is active in a wide range of charitable and civic organizations, including the Joslin Diabetes Foundation, the Statue of Liberty-Ellis Island Foundation, Reading Is Fundamental, and The Iacocca Foundation. Iacocca is the author of two best-selling books, *Iacocca* and *Talking Straight,* and writes a nationally syndicated newspaper column.

JOHN VASCONCELLOS

♥

"Our peaceful existence with each other is inextricably linked to the peace we feel in our own beings."

The reason that we have so little peace and love in our world today is not because of lack of desire, but because of lack of awareness about how to realize our innate human inclinations toward becoming constructive, life affirming, responsible, and trustworthy individuals. We need to learn how to be loving, peace-making beings. Each of us must commit himself or herself now, to learn how to foster individual self-esteem, well-being, and the capacity to lead a responsible, loving, and peace-making life.

Our peaceful existence with each other is inextricably linked to the peace we feel in our own beings. When we are not secure in our beings and are not sure of our individual worth and self-esteem, we often compensate for situations and people that threaten us by seeking power or control over them. We behave in harmful ways toward each other as a result of our own insecurities.

Self-esteem at its core is our innate feeling of well-being and contentment, which expresses itself in common sense and service to others. S̲elf-E̲steem E̲ngenders P̲eace and will *seep* into every corner of our globe as we awaken to the importance of respecting our own worth, and therefore each and every other person's worth. We then need to interact with each other on that basis.

The key to world peace lies within ourselves, and in realizing our ability to become compassionate and warm people, who altogether celebrate our presence and our partnership in making our world more loving and peaceful. This is no act of selfishness; selfish people fail to accept the responsibility and devote the energy to serving others; the whole and self-esteeming people are spontaneously there—loving and making peace!

———♥———

John Vasconcellos is serving his thirteenth term representing the twenty-third Assembly District (Santa Clara County/Silicon Valley) in the California legislature. Vasconcellos is the founder of California's Task Force on Self-Esteem and Personal and Social Responsibility and serves on the assembly education and higher education committees. His primary concerns are to encourage the development of healthy, self-realizing human beings and concentrate on issues affecting human development and personal and social responsibility. The author of *A Liberating Vision: Politics for Growing Humans,* he personally invites you to join him as a partner in these endeavors.

BARBARA DE ANGELIS

♥

"It starts with you, creating peace in your relationships by resolving anger, blame, and bitterness; creating peace within yourself by embracing, forgiving, and celebrating all the parts of you including your inner child; creating peace in society by looking for ways to show your love and caring to the people you meet."

YOUR LOVE MAKES A DIFFERENCE

It's impossible to live on this planet and not ask yourself, "What am I doing here? What is my purpose? How can I give my life meaning?" Sometimes when we ask the question, we don't get an answer, so we bury ourselves in what appear to be useful activities: making money, taking vacations, redecorating our homes. And life becomes a process of filling in time, rather than finding ultimate meaning. And some people run away with the question altogether, using alcohol, drugs, work, whatever they can find, to avoid looking in the mirror.

As a teacher and a seeker, these questions echo through my mind every day. As for me, the process of answering them includes using my gifts to encourage other people to ask the same questions, and guiding them toward some possible answers.

I believe life's purpose is simply to celebrate ourselves, our existence, and, especially, the experience of sharing love with one another. This gives meaning to everything. Without love, life is very empty and mechanical. But experiencing the simplest event with love turns it into something wonderful and exciting, whether it's love of one special person, love of yourself, love of nature, or love of God. And then life is never boring. Through the eyes of love, the same person's face, the same sunset, the same mountain look beautiful and glorious every single time. I can't imagine how anyone can truly look at our physical world and not see that it was made from and of love. And I feel our purpose here is to come back to a state in which we all experience that.

Sometimes we observe the media and become depressed because we feel helpless to change the suffering we see around us. "There's nothing I can do that will make a difference," each person thinks, "It's that person who is in charge, or those people who make the rules. They're the ones with the power to do something." So we decide to live our lives oblivious to what is going on around us because we feel impotent, and we become self-absorbed and wonder why we feel purposeless.

Peace is not a political reality. Peace is a spiritual reality that begins inside of each person in the loving space of his or her own heart that emanates out, affecting everyone around that person. Peace cannot be legislated—it can only spring from each individual who has found peace within. That's why I say that peace begins at home. Perhaps you can't do anything right now to affect the masses on a large scale, but if you decided to create peace in your own life, emotionally and spiritually, and if everyone else made that same decision, our planet would change drastically.

I know people who claim to be making a difference in the world by developing programs, or changing the educational system, or working for social reform, who then constantly turn to their own children and yell at them, or neglect their spouse, or refuse to talk about their feelings and walk around with suppressed anger and hostility. I don't call that a peacemaker. I call that a warmaker.

If you have a fight with someone you love, and storm out of the house without resolving it, that is war. You get to your office and snap at your coworkers. You are impatient on the phone with your clients. You walk to lunch exuding negative energy. Do you realize how many people you have just affected, and how many people each of them will affect? Each of us has such a profound effect upon thousands of people each week without knowing it. And it's a chain that doesn't just go in one direction—it spreads out in concentric circles so that your smile can affect thousands of people over the course of an hour, and so can your frown.

Your choice to love makes an incredible difference in the world. That means choosing to make a difference by the way you treat yourself, your loved ones, and the people you come into contact with. It starts with you, creating peace in your relationships by resolving anger, blame, and bitterness; creating peace within yourself by embracing, forgiving, and celebrating all the parts of you including your inner child; creating peace in society by looking for ways to show your love and caring to the people you meet. It means encouraging your best friend to heal his or her marriage instead of constantly listening to that person complain about it. It means seeing the perfect spirit in your children and letting them know you see it, instead of only giving them feedback when they do something wrong. It means loving enough to speak out.

I have an image that one day when our lives on earth end, we ascend to a higher plane of existence and are interviewed by God. I don't believe that God would ask each of us, "How much money did you gross in 1992?" or "How many cars did you own?" or "Did you ever get rid of all the cellulite?" I imagine that God would ask, "How well did you love? How much joy did you create in the people around you? How much did you love and appreciate yourself, your body, and your own special gift? How many hearts did you touch?"

That's what making a difference means. It means asking yourself daily, "How well did I love?" Then you become someone who is contributing your own gift to our planet. Then you feel like you belong here. Then you feel like you are really home.

Barbara De Angelis, Ph.D., is a widely respected relationships expert and media personality who has earned the title of "The Love Doctor" by members of the press. Dr. De Angelis is the executive director of the Los Angeles Personal Growth Center, as well as the creator of the relationships seminar "Making Love Work." Author of two best-selling books, *How to Make Love All the Time* and *Secrets About Men Every Woman Should Know,* De Angelis teaches and lectures extensively around the world at conventions, conferences, and symposia. Her next book, *Are You the One for Me?,* will be in the bookstores soon.

CASEY KASEM

♥

"Compassion is the ultimate ethic."

Of all the various concerns I have and support actively, I'd have to say my number one priority is doing what I can to convince people to become *vegetarians*. Here's why. Many people feel they have no power to make a difference. But the easiest way to *become* empowered and help change the world is to become a vegetarian. This has an impact in three areas simultaneously: ecology, health, and ethics.

Too many Americans die each year from poor diets, loaded with animal fats, cholesterol, you name it. A better diet can mean a longer, healthier life. Why kill animals for food when we can get all the nutrients we need from fruit, seeds, nuts, and vegetables?

Someone once said that by becoming vegetarian, "your body will respect you for your wisdom, and the animals will love you for your compassion." Compassion is the ultimate ethic. It's likely that world peace will have its roots in a nonviolent diet. So, save your health, save the animals, and save our earth. Become a vegetarian now. You *can* make a difference in the world by first making a difference in yourself.

Millions of fans around the world find the name Casey Kasem synonymous with musical countdowns. He now celebrates his twenty-second year of counting down the hits on radio, currently with "Casey's Top 40, with Casey Kasem" on the Westwood One network, as well as his twelfth year of doing the same on television, with "America's Top Ten." A character actor and veteran of countless voice-over commercials and Saturday morning cartoon shows, Kasem is also involved in many social and humanitarian causes, from anti-smoking campaigns to anti-discrimination projects. His abiding concern has been to help bring about peace and an end to the nuclear threat.

DEAN MARTIN

Like the song, "The Nearness of You," you can love someone, but most important, you have to like that person. Then you'll make a difference in the world.

Since his television debut in 1957, Dean Martin has been charming audiences for over forty years. A singer, actor, and comedian, Martin has starred in over fifty-one motion pictures, including *Who's That Sleeping in My Bed?*, *Robin and the Seven Hoods, Airport,* and *The Cannonball Run,* in addition to the popular Matt Helms films. He still occasionally hosts one of his famous "Dean Martin Roasts."

DELLA REESE

♥

"I can make a difference by caring, by 'loving my neighbor as I love myself.'"

We tend to look for the large solutions to our challenges, like making a difference in the world, and overlook the seed or core that we need to make the solution's foundation strong. The solution must grow firm and strong and its foundation must support that growth.

Jesus answered this question a long time ago. He said, "Thou shall love thy neighbor as thyself." Some of you reading this may say we need new politicians, new legislation, money sources that will do this or that, and we probably do; but if we *really* cared we would have them. So we must not *really* care. If we did we couldn't rest without them.

On the other hand, if we followed Jesus' idea, things would be different because the pattern would be different. I don't know how you feel but I like me a lot. I believe that only the exceptional best is good enough for me. According to Christ that is how I am suppose to love my neighbor, like myself.

I like to sleep warm, eat well, create, laugh long with good reason. Feel good, feel joyous, feel loved, and I am about getting these things all the time. If I loved my neighbor as myself I'd want my neighbor to have these things also. I couldn't enjoy mine knowing my neighbor was without. You know how it is, and how you act, when you love someone or something.

This planet is our home and we are all neighbors. Some of us live closer together than others. Some live next door and some live across the world, still, we are all neighbors, for what one does affects the rest of us. I must love all my neighbors, not just next door or in my community. It is true I cannot feed all the hungry nor provide beds for all of those without shelter. I can feed one or two. I can give help to someone to get a place to sleep. I cannot stop a war but I can give comfort to someone that a war has touched, by sharing the peace and love within me. I share this love with my neighbor, whomever my neighbor may be, whether he or she is someone I've known forever, or someone I pass in the street who needs my help.

I can stand for peace in my own world and invite my neighbors into my world to share that peace as often as possible. I can look past the faults of my neighbor and deal with the good and not become another problem for him or her. I can listen. I can give myself. I can be positive instead of negative. I can make a difference by caring, by "loving my neighbor as I love myself." Then I will get the right legislation, politicians, world leaders, money sources, and whatever else the world needs. And when my brothers love me as they love themselves it will be done worldwide. Each person has to start with himself or herself.

A jazz-blues-gospel singer, composer, and actress, Della Reese has been entertaining audiences for over twenty years. Starting her television career on television sitcoms in the seventies and eighties, Reese is now focusing on her action and dramatic talents, and has recently been featured in many television shows, including "A Team," "Young Riders," "MacGyver," and "Nightmare in Badham County," for which she was nominated for an Emmy award. Reese is an ordained minister through the Universal Foundation for Better Living, an organization of twenty-two churches worldwide, and holds services at her church in Southern California.

JERRY GILLIES

♥

"... when people get as excited about peace as they do about war, as attached to love as they are to hate, revenge, and bigotry, then the whole planet will make that leap to the next level of human evolution."

Not only is it becoming easier for one individual to make a real impact on the world, but it is becoming more vital for individuals to make a real effort in this area. The good news is that this is happening, with ever-increasing numbers of people committed to changing the planet for the better. Never before in human history have more people been more concerned with issues of peace, ecology, health, human rights, animal rights, and the right of everyone alive to have happiness and prosperity.

When people attend my seminars on creating success and prosperity they are often surprised at how much emphasis I place on loving and serving others. In fact, I assert that should an individual choose to have as his or her primary focus the task of learning to become a more loving and serving person, all other needs and desires would be taken care of.

The business that spreads love and peace will reap greater profits as we move into the twenty-first century. And the individual who does business while focusing on loving and serving will attract lots more response from the marketplace. One caution here: I feel it's important that an individual doesn't just "do" love and peace. In other words, each individual should have something he or she is passionate about doing in the world, and use that as a vehicle for spreading love and peace.

The easiest way for someone to make a difference is to become a shining example to others. We saw this in the citizen diplomacy movement of the past fifteen years, which had its most notable impact in the Soviet Union and Eastern Europe. The Berlin Wall came down not through protest, not through revolution, and not through people preaching peace and love. It came down as the direct result of a burning desire on the part of the East Germans to have a quality of life they saw in the West, both through the eyes of western visitors and via television from the West. The information and media explosion have made the world too small and too wise for anyone to believe lies from a despotic regime for very long. One American or Dane or Canadian telling the truth about freedom of choice and expression and economic opportunity to a new friend who has very limited amounts of these things sets off a chain reaction of robust expectations. And when people get as excited about peace as they do about war, as attached to love as they are to hate, revenge, and bigotry, then the whole planet will make that leap to the next level of human evolution.

Jerry Gillies is the author of six books on self-development, including the 1.3 million-copy best-seller *Moneylove*. A former NBC newsman and business reporter, Gillies has been conducting public and corporate seminars on creativity, communication, and prosperity since 1971 in the United States, England, Europe, Africa, and Canada. Gillies, former founding director of the Biofeedback Institute, serves on the board of advisors of The Inside Edge leadership group along with Dr. Wayne Dyer, Dr. Nathaniel Branden, and Dennis Weaver.

KATHY HILTON

♥

Making a difference in the world includes being positive, having a smile on your face, being an honest person, a good friend, and a good mother, father, brother, or sister. People need to understand where other people are coming from, walk in their shoes. Not be judgmental. Not expect everyone to look at things or view things the way they want them to. Trust. Be a listener. Not be so critical, but look for the good. Be grateful. Stop and smell the roses. Be thankful and positive and thank God every day for their blessings.

―♥―

Kathy Hilton is the president of The Gems, the fundraising arm for the Pacific Multiple Sclerosis Research Foundation, which raises funds for research at UCLA. The wife of Rick Hilton, president of Hilton Realty Investment and son of Barron Hilton of Hilton Hotels, Ms. Hilton is also involved in many charities, including SHARE. Hilton is also the owner of the Los Angeles boutique, The Staircase.

GARY ZUKAV

"Fundamental change must now come from within. All other change is superficial."

To make the world different than it is now, we must become different than we are now. There is no other way to accomplish social, political, or economic change at a fundamental level.

The orientations that have produced the social, political, and economic structures of humankind will not produce different structures in the future. They will only produce more of the same.

More of the same is not now sufficient. "Business as usual" has not only become counterproductive, it has become destructive. Poverty, hunger, suffering, and brutality are expanding everywhere. This is not the consequence of ailing economies. "Ailing" economies themselves are a consequence of a deeper cause that is affecting every human on the Earth, and every social, political, and economic structure that now exists.

Our species has entered a new phase of its evolution that has no precedent. We are no longer evolving through the exploration of physical reality. We are now evolving through responsible choice with the assistance and guidance of nonphysical guides and Teachers. This change in the modality of our evolution is momentous. Nothing in the history of humanity compares with it, except Genesis. This is a new Genesis: the birth of the human species into new dimensions of experience and awareness.

We are also leaving behind the limitations of the five senses. We are becoming a species that is no longer confined to the experiences of those things that can be seen, heard, tasted, touched, and smelled. The domain of the five senses has been our learning environment for hundreds of thousands of years. Now we are moving into a larger domain.

While we were confined to the experiences of the five senses, we learned through acquiring the ability to manipulate and control our environment, and others. This is a type of power: power over those things that appear to be external. It is external power. It is the perception of power that is appropriate to a species that is limited to the perceptions of the five senses. Learning through the exploration of physical reality and acquiring external power are identical.

As we move beyond the limitations of the five senses, individual after individual after individual is acquiring the perception of himself or herself as an immortal soul. Individual by individual, we are becoming able to distinguish the difference between personality and soul, and to identify ourselves as immortal souls, and not time-limited personalities. We are discovering that the deepest hungers within us can only be satisfied by striving to align our personalities with our souls, and as we begin the process of doing that, we are coming to a new perception and definition of power—*authentic power.*

Authentic power comes from aligning your personality with your soul. It is very different from external power—the ability to control and manipulate. It cannot be lost, stolen, inherited, or won. It is the experience of being completely engaged in the present moment, fulfilled and fulfilling. It is the feeling that comes with giving yourself entirely in joy to what you are doing. It is the satisfaction of knowing why you are born, what your purpose in life is, and doing it. It is a knowing of the heart that needs no proof and cannot be disproved.

Attaining authentic power—the alignment of the personality with the soul—is not easy, just as gaining external power was not easy. It requires responsible choice. The soul reaches always toward harmony, cooperation, sharing, and reverence for Life. When you are challenged by your anger, jealously, anxiety, fear, and despair, and yet in those moments choose words and actions that move toward creating harmony where there was discord, cooperation where there was competition, sharing where there was hoarding, and reverence for Life where there was disregard for Life, you move toward authentic power. This is how authentic power is gained: choice by choice, step by step. It cannot be wished, prayed, meditated, or talked into being. It must be earned.

As we move beyond the five senses, we are able to engage in this process with the assistance of nonphysical guides and Teachers. Our hunches about particular actions, circumstances, and individuals become important. Our intuition becomes more and more central in our decision making. We strive to become aware of what we feel, take those feelings inward, and decide. This is how we begin the process of becoming conscious of the nonphysical guidance and assistance that is always with us. We realize that we are not alone, that it is impossible to be alone. We realize that the Universe is alive, that there is nothing in the Universe that is not alive, and that we are a part of the living Universe.

This is the course on which humankind is now embarked: the pursuit of authentic power—the alignment of the personality with the soul—through the mechanism of responsible choice with the assistance and guidance of nonphysical guides and Teachers.

All of our current political, social, and economic structures are based upon the perception of power as external, as the ability to manipulate and control. That is why they are not working. The script has been changed, but the old scenery is still on the stage. It is in the process of being removed and replaced. It will no longer suffice to make improvements on the old scenery, or replace it with more of the same. Its purpose has been accomplished, and a new play has begun.

Fundamental change must now come from within. All other change is superficial. One political party, for example, can be voted out and another voted in (one looses external power to another that gains it), but the change is not fundamental. The political structure that is based upon the perception of power as external remains in place. This is what lies behind the apathy of voters in mature democracies: the emotional realization that engaging in this process does not bring about change.

The homogeneity of the candidates that present themselves, despite the varying positions that they assume, results from the commonality that they share: all are pursuing external power. They are seeking the ability to manipulate and control while the humankind that is emerging longs for ways to cooperate, share, create in harmony, and honor life.

The circumstance cannot be changed through legislation—more control and manipulation by those who, for the moment, have gained the external power to legislate; nor through the courts—established to impede the ability of government to control and manipulate unhindered; nor through executive decree. It reflects perfectly the advanced state of a species that has evolved through the exploration of physical reality, and has mastered its understanding of external power. It will change naturally as humanity moves through the transition from a species that pursues external power to a species that pursues authentic power. That transition is longing to be born within each human. It is up to each individual, responsible choice by responsible choice, to give it birth. No one else can do it.

Our economy, national and global, reflects the perception of power as external. Money, like external power, is seen as belonging to a few whom the rest serve as victims. Our economic thinking and structures are based upon the assumption of scarcity, and our economic activities are designed to exploit others and the Earth. Competition for capital, markets, and resources determines economic success, which is measured by the accumulation of surplus—called profit—or the lack of it. This arena of human endeavor reflects with precision the perception of power that has been held by the human species until now—power as the ability to manipulate and control.

This picture will change as humankind changes. It cannot be changed in any other way. As the understanding of power as the ability to manipulate and control is challenged and replaced by the understanding of power as the alignment of the personality with the soul, a new economy will emerge that is based upon the assumption of abundance and oriented toward contribution. Cooperation will replace competition, and the economy that is seeking to be born, as it comes into being, will strive to contribute to Life rather than to exploit Life. This cannot happen while individual humans live with the assumption of scarcity, seek security in competition rather than cooperation, and strive to exploit Life rather than to contribute to it.

The depth of the extraordinary transformation in which we are engaged is profound and exciting. The existence of individual humans as immortal souls learning within the arena of the five senses is coming into the awareness of our species for the first time on a species-wide scale. With it is coming awareness of the power of individual human consciousness—the ability to choose responsible—and the relationship of human choices to the five-sensory world in which we live.

What shall we choose now?

Gary Zukav is the winner of the 1979 American Book Award in Science for *The Dancing Wu Li Masters,* and author of *The Seat of the Soul.* A graduate of Harvard University, Zukav lives in Northern California.

LEONARD ORR

❤

We can spread love and peace by doing something practical. Until love and peace permeate politics and economics, it is just an airy, fairy theory or a feeling. Work is love made visible. The ideas of neighborhood representation, government without taxes, and physical immortality through spiritual purification with earth, air, water, and fire are essential to love and peace. Political suppression, economic bondage, and the death of the body make peace and love difficult, temporary, and ephemeral.

Starter of the Conscious Energy Breathing (Rebirthing) Movement, which has since spread to over 10 million people, Leonard Orr began studying life extension and longevity in 1961, which he calls simply, "physical immortality." Orr is the author of four books on physical immortality, in addition to *Rebirthing in the New Age,* which he coauthored with Sondra Ray.

KEN NORTON

♥

If you believe in yourself and you believe in God, you will have inner peace. When you have inner peace you will make a difference.

———♦———

Ken Norton shocked the boxing world in 1973 when he defeated former heavyweight champion Muhammad Ali in a twelve-round bout, breaking Ali's jaw and gaining a name for himself as a fighter with a will of steel. Norton fought his way through the ranks to become the world boxing champion of the WBC in 1978 and holds a career record of thirty-two bouts and twenty-two knockouts. Following his retirement from professional boxing in 1981, Ken opened the Norton Novelty Company, a supplier of Olympic memorabilia, opened his own sports management company, and made many feature film and television appearances. Today, Norton operates his own health club facility, and is proud to say that the second of his five children, Ken, Jr., plays football for the Dallas Cowboys.

THOMAS H. JUSTIN

"Our contributions, positive or negative, are always significant, whether we give lip service to world peace, then react in anger, or create peace within, then act accordingly. We can only control our actions; the consequences of those actions are beyond our reach or realm."

THE CONSEQUENCE OF PEACE

The freeway traffic was surprisingly light for a midweek day. I was tuning my radio when the sudden blast of a car horn startled me. My head snapped to the left just in time to realize that I had been drifting toward the other lane. Relieved that it was nothing more serious, I waved my hand contritely to the other driver, both as an apology and a thank-you for being more diligent than I.

The car horn continued to blare as the driver came even with me. As he paced me, still honking his horn, I looked to my left being mindful of the news reports of freeway shootings. He appeared to be well-dressed and neatly groomed in an American-made midsize car. If we were to see this man under normal circumstances we might visualize him as a middle class manager, married, with 2.3 kids. But these were not normal circumstances.

As I slowed, he slowed. His jaw, in furious motion, jutted in my direction. A visual, but unheard, anger was being projected at me, buffered between two panes of safety glass. Like a silent movie without the need for subtitles, he continued on, alternately shaking his fist and honking his horn.

I shrugged my shoulders as if to say, "I'm sorry, I made a mistake." This seemed to enrage him more and his soundless jaw motion intensified. With a look of ferociousness he extended his arm with an unmistakable hand signal, sometimes known as the freeway salute. Finally, he accelerated, his head bobbing and weaving and his hands pounding on the steering wheel. Relieved, I watched the car fade into the traffic. The last thing I saw was his bumper sticker proclaiming Support World Peace.

When I stopped laughing I realized what a good analogy and lesson this was for me. I thought how my inner peace, or lack of it, has affected the level of peace elsewhere in my world. My relationships are more volatile and tempers flare easily when I'm not at peace with myself. When I feel peaceful, I react in a peaceful way, even to events such as that poor man and his horn. "How many months or years," I wondered, "were subtracted from his life because of his extreme reactions?" I realized the frequency of my overreactions in similar circumstances, both in inner and outer displays of anger and impatience.

I recalled a lecture on astronomy years ago, and how the speaker described the make up of the universe. The relationship of our cells to our organs, and how trauma in one area affects another was an analogy that occurred to me. The human body is simply another form of universe. The idea of holistic healing, treating the whole body instead of the symptoms, seems applicable to our earth and universe. Each action creates a consequence or reaction of which we have no control.

The Frank Capra movie, *It's a Wonderful Life,* with Jimmy Stewart, is a good example of the consequence of action. Stewart's character got to see what his small world would be like had he never lived. His seemingly insignificant life was extraordinarily significant. The consequences of our actions always manifest a domino effect. All action is power, and it is our awareness, or lack of it, that guides us toward the constructive use of that power.

Our contributions, positive or negative, are always significant, whether we give lip service to world peace, then react in anger, or create peace within, then act accordingly. We can only control our actions; the consequences of those actions are beyond our reach or realm. We must come to know the power within us. When our actions consistently create inner peace, the consequence will be world peace. A consequence of peace, can only be more peace.

Perhaps our bumper stickers should read Support Inner Peace.

―♥―

Thomas H. Justin has been a professional communicator for over twenty years, speaking to and training thousands of people on the subject of personal growth and relationships. The cornerstone of Justin's speeches and seminars is the tremendous personal power that resides in each of us and a person's ability to manifest it. A professional whose life has encompassed journalism, entertainment, speaking, and writing, Justin applies his techniques to all forms of relationships in his book and audio tape series, *Relationship Breakthroughs*. He is currently working on his second book, *How to Take No for an Answer and Still Succeed*.

JAMIE SAMS

"I have come to know that we are one planet, one people, and that every human being has the same basic needs and desires."

When I was asked to write what my philosophy on life was and how my personal knowing system could make a difference in the world, I was suddenly at a loss since our Native American knowing systems are a way of living and being connected. I had to look at the sacredness with which each part of creation worked in harmony inside of me, as well as in the outer world, in order to renew my perspective as an individual.

Dignity is the divine right of every life form on the earth and each part of creation has what is called a sacred space. Inside the sacred space each living thing has a sacred point of view. From these innumerable points of view, we, as human beings, perceive the total reality of physical life and our perfect place within the whole. Everything is alive. Everything has a purpose. The joy of life's journey is in discovery and I decided to enjoy that adventure by honoring every step along the way. I chose to learn the languages of the trees, stones, animals, and elements in order to find my place in the whole.

The separation that has kept humankind from acknowledging the common ground is fast slipping into past history as we issue in the fifth world of peace and illumination that was foretold by my ancestors. The dignity of every life form is being renewed and the consciousness of humankind is returning. I feel that I am blessed to be an ordinary human living in extraordinary times. I am like every other human on earth. I feel, I breathe, I reason, I take action, and I retreat in order to regroup. I laugh, I cry, and I love. I know that eventually I will slip from my body and cross into the spirit world. I have seen this same humanness across the planet in the faces of every race and culture. I have come to know that we are one planet, one people, and that every human being has the same basic needs and desires. Every person has something to contribute to the whole even if that talent is undiscovered or not fully developed. I know in my heart that every individual is able to make a difference in our world.

My personal journey is to share new role models or blueprints for humankind to use in order to find inner peace. These life maps combine the ancient knowledge of harmony with all our relations with modern ways to reclaim the love of life. Finding new ways for myself and others to express our unique talents in order to contribute to the whole is my life work. My family impressed upon me that every person has the ability to accomplish anything he or she sets his or her mind to if that person makes it a priority. Nothing is ever impossible if we maintain our connection to the great mystery, the earth mother, and treat all life with dignity and respect.

Jamie Sams is an author and Native American medicine teacher who lives in northern New Mexico. She has written five books, including *The Sacred Path Cards, The Discovery of Self Through Native Teachings, Other Council Fires Were Here Before Ours,* and *The Sacred Path Card Workbook.* Her main life purpose is connecting the past to the present in order to broaden the public viewpoint regarding the history of earth.

She has worked on retrieving records from Africa, Egypt, Mexico, England, Peru, Guatemala, and the United States. Her personal goal is to reeducate humankind so that we may become one planet—one people.

SHAKTI GAWAIN

"If we truly intend to spread love and peace in the world it can only be done by seeking to know, accept, and love all aspects of ourselves, including the parts of ourselves that aren't loving and peaceful—our fear, our need, our anger and hate."

Every one of us does make a difference in spreading love and peace in the world to the degree that one is truly committed to one's own growth process. Because the mass consciousness is made up on many individuals, as any individual consciousness shifts it affects the whole—more powerfully than most of us realize. A relatively small number of people with a new level of awareness creates rapid change in the world.

A true commitment to one's own journey of conscious evolution, however, requires courage. It's far easier to focus on the external problems of the world, or other people's problems, and try to fix them. To face oneself, and seek to truly know oneself is very challenging, and at times can be quite frightening. To make this journey we must be willing to go through the scary, confusing times as well as the high, exciting moments.

In order to become conscious individuals in a conscious world, we must heal and integrate all levels of our being—spiritual, mental, emotional, and physical. There are many people around these days who are happy to do the work on the spiritual level because it feels good and makes them high, or on the mental level because it feels safer and more familiar. Far fewer are willing to get down and do the deep healing work on the emotional/psychological level, because that's where one has to face one's shadow—all the aspects of oneself and of life that have been disowned, repressed, or avoided. Until we've embraced all parts of ourselves and integrated them in our lives we can't function in a whole and healthy way on the physical plane.

The physical plane is a plane of duality—in this world all things exist as pairs of opposites. True consciousness involves accepting all the polarities within us. Whatever one rejects, or tries to get rid of, increases in power. Whatever one accepts becomes a natural, harmonious part of the whole picture.

The popular wisdom about how to spread love and peace in the world is to "be a more loving and peaceful person." Many people are trying to be "unconditionally loving," and are joining together to meditate and visualize peace. This is all very well, but it's only one side of the coin. The paradox is, to find inner peace and create outer peace we have to accept and feel comfortable with our aggression as well. Aggression, while it can be misused, in essence is not a negative thing. When expressed in a healthy form it's simply the ability to use our power to achieve what we want in life.

Most people on a so-called "spiritual" path repress their aggression and become very identified with their passive energies, which they perceive as more virtuous. But repressed energies do not disappear. They are inevitably expressed somewhere in our lives and in our world, usually in a very negative, distorted form. So a person who has disowned aggression may then become a victim of aggression, or perhaps the "victim" of an aggressive disease.

Disowning aggression actually supports aggression on a mass level. Owning healthy aggression and allowing it to take its natural place in life helps one feel at peace with oneself and promotes peace in the world.

If we truly intend to spread love and peace in the world it can only be done by seeking to know, accept, and love all aspects of ourselves, including the parts of ourselves that aren't loving and peaceful—our fear, our need, our anger and hate. Thus we can embrace and embody, in peace and with passion, all of life.

Shakti Gawain is the best-selling author of *Creative Visualization, Living in the Light, Reflections in the Light, Return to the Garden,* and *Awakening,* and the co-founder of New World Library Publishing Company. A warm, articulate, and inspiring teacher, Gawain leads workshops internationally. In the past twelve years she has facilitated thousands of people in learning to trust and act on their own inner truth, thus releasing and developing their creativity in every area of their lives.

Alice Billings

DENNIS WEAVER

♥

In the decade of the nineties, we are challenged to understand, as individuals, our connectedness with all other living things, to clean up our inner environment, so that ultimately our actions spring from love . . . the lack of which is the root cause of all our problems. For whatever we are within, we will reflect outwardly.

———♥———

Dennis Weaver, actor, humanitarian, and environmental activist, has been in the public eye four decades. Whether helping feed the hungry, speaking for world peace, or taking a stand on healing the earth, by his example and commitment he inspires others to help bring about a shift towards oneness and love. Weaver is co-founder and working president of LIFE (Love Is Feeding Everyone), a community-activated food distribution program in Los Angeles, and a member of the board of directors of ECO (Earth Communications Office), a group of people from the entertainment industry who are dedicated to saving the planet.

BRIAN TRACY

♥

The very best way to make a difference in the world is by example. Start by setting yourself up as a role model and continually ask, "What kind of a world would my world be if everyone in it were just like me?" This question imposes on us a higher standard of morality and behavior. It forces us to rise above the petty emotions of animosity and revenge, and give more careful consideration to the secondary consequences of our actions. If every person were to accept full responsibility for what might happen as a result of what he or she said or did, each person would more often tend to say and do things that would spread more love and peace in the world.

―♥―

Brian Tracy is one of America's leading speakers on the development of human potential and personal effectiveness, who addresses hundreds of thousands of men and women each year on the subjects of leadership, strategic planning, organizational development, creativity, self-esteem, goal setting, success psychology, and time management. The author of several best-selling audio and video-based training programs and the president of Brian Tracy Learning Systems Inc., a human resource company based in San Diego, California, Tracy has had successful careers in sales, marketing, advertising, investments, real estate development, and syndication, importation, distribution, and management consulting for a broad spectrum of industries. As a consultant, Brian has trained key executives of more than one thousand corporations in the United States, Canada, Mexico, the Far East, Australia, and Europe.

FRANK H.T. RHODES

♥

We live not only in a global village of bewildering allegiances, but in a multicultural nation, and while we shall never outgrow the teachings of Jesus and Moses, we need to learn also from Mohammed, Buddha, and Gandhi because the values for which they stood continue to motivate and inspire millions. Proud as we should be of our differences in heritage and commitment as a source of individual identity, there remains a level on which we need to function as a community if we are to survive. That may be the toughest challenge facing our generation.

Frank H.T. Rhodes is the ninth president of Cornell University. A geologist by training, he was appointed in 1977 and also holds the faculty rank of professor of geology at Cornell. He is the author of over seventy major scientific articles and monographs, over sixty articles on education, and five books.

CHRISTINE BINGHAM COTÉ
♥

"The love that brings peace is more than just 'a feeling of warm personal attachment or deep affection.' A feeling of love needs to transform into 'actions of love.'"

Spreading "love and peace" was one of the motivating factors my daughter Cheryl and I had for entering the Mother/Daughter Pageant. One of the questions on the application was "Why do you want to enter the Mother/Daughter Pageant?" Part of my answer was "The pageant would enable us to exchange some of our ideas, love, and concerns with others." For several years we were touched as we watched other mothers and daughters in the pageant. We, too, wanted to share the love, compassion, concern, and encouragement we saw expressed in the eyes, words, and hugs of those in the pageant. What better way than through the modern wonder of television media could I share my conviction that being a good parent is the greatest responsibility and most important occupation of a lifetime on this planet?

As I have looked around our earth at the uneven distribution of pain and comfort, happiness and sorrow, problems and joys, my heart has gone out to those who have less than I. I've asked myself, "What can I do to help?" The answer that keeps coming back to me is "Take care of my own family first." That seems like such a small contribution to make toward my great desire of "fixing the whole world." If only there was a way to convince everyone that the bottom line is to act with love!

My motherly instinct tells me that peace would dominate this planet if only all parents could communicate love! One of my sons taught me this lesson in a very short sentence one day when I was philosophizing. He had been in junior high and high school during the apex of drug use in California by teenagers. He had had his problems and frustrations, like most teenagers have. He was surrounded by friends who experimented with drugs to a greater or lesser degree, and he possessed a strong curiosity. When he was in college (on this day when I was philosophizing), I asked him, "Eric, what kept you from getting into drugs?" His reply was simply, "It would have killed you!" That is love! How comforted I felt that his love for me proved stronger than the pressures of his troubles, his peers, or his curiosity. He cared about my happiness more than his own!

My definition of love goes beyond that of Webster's definition. The love that brings peace is more than just "a feeling of warm personal attachment or deep affection." A feeling of love needs to transform into "actions of love." I have a very simple definition of "actions of love": very unselfish actions of true concern for another's best interests. The people that exhibit "actions of love" place the needs of others before their own personal needs. I am not a great psychologist or erudite, but many great teachers, such as Jesus Christ, Confucius, Mohammed, Buddha, and Lao-tzu, have filled books about how to "act with love and peace," about how to care for another's needs.

Learning how to "act lovingly" can first be learned at home. It must be understood and practiced on a daily basis. Since feelings can only be "perceived," it is very important that parents are able to convey their feelings of love. It does a child little good to have a loving parent who is unable to convince or show a child how much he or she loves the child. Unfortunately, I once heard that the easiest way to learn to be a good parent is to have had good parents. Many of us were not fortunate enough to have been blessed with good parents. But, thank God, we can learn! However, it amazes me that there are few classes or training centers on being a good parent—the most important job and greatest responsibility of a lifetime! Isn't that shocking? That tells me our society has not given loving behavior or parental responsibilities a very high position on our priority lists.

That brings me back to the reason I appreciated the Mother/Daughter Pageant. I know the promotion of love and good parental relationships was not the motivating factor in producing the pageant, but I love the results it had of recognizing and rewarding behavior that is so beneficial to our society. Parents, teachers, peers, and leaders of our country have emphasized winning, achieving, owning material possessions, learning all kinds of things other than how to be a good parent, and the priority list goes on, before they emphasize loving behavior or good parenting. It's about time we recognize and reward "being a good parent" by being able to "act with love." The results will be living in a world of peace!

As a full-time mom, tax specialist, and community organization leader, Christine Bingham Coté discovered that no job or responsibility in this world can compare to that of raising children. Fortunately, the rewards are as great as the responsibilities—one of her life's most delightful experiences was winning the 1989/1990 California Mother/Daughter Pageant hand-in-hand with her daughter, Cheryl, where they had a unique opportunity to exchange some of their ideas, love, and concerns with the world. Bingham Coté is married to Greenpeace founder Paul Coté, and lives, loves, and laughs with him in Rancho Santa Fe, California.

ARNOLD M. PATENT

♥

"... when we support one another, we really support ourselves."

It's great to feel inspired! We have more energy. We feel more alive. When do we feel inspired? We feel inspired when we connect with the part of ourselves that knows that our lives are purposeful—that there is a lot more to our lives than just getting through each day.

How do we find this purpose? One of the ways we connect with it is when we are part of an experience that lifts us above our ordinary ways of seeing our lives. Many of us connected with the inspiration of our purpose when we listened to the Live Aid concert, heard the playing of "America the Beautiful" during our Bicentennial Celebration, or watched John F. Kennedy exhort us to ask not what our country can do for us, but what can we do for our country.

What these events have in common is that they help us see that when we come together to improve the quality of life for each other, we feel wonderful. This is what purpose is all about—the willingness to define our lives in terms that are universal enough for us to feel connected. It is the willingness to open to the part of ourselves that knows that life is really a mutual support process—that when we support one another, we really support ourselves.

As we recognize that indeed there is a purpose to our lives, it is easier to connect with it. We can sit quietly and ask the part of us that is aware of our purpose to share it. We know that we are hearing correctly when we feel inspired by what we hear. Connecting with our purpose is a feeling experience. And we access our feelings through our hearts. Therefore, it is important that we open our hearts before we ask. It is also important to remember that in order to stay infused with the inspiration of our purpose, we must keep our hearts open.

When we combine the inspiration of our purpose with the power that we access through our hearts, we stimulate our creativity. Combining all three, inspiration of purpose, open-heart power, and creativity, leads to activities that benefit everyone.

After a highly successful twenty-five-year career as a practicing attorney, investor, and financial advisor, Arnold M. Patent began a new lifestyle—that of author, teacher, and seminar leader. Patent found some very basic truths that, when adhered to, afforded him the opportunity to be supportive of everyone with whom he came into contact. The practice of these truths, which he calls Universal Principles, so enriched his life that he decided to share them in his seminars and his book, *You Can Have It All*. Patent, a keynote speaker who has appeared on many television and radio talk shows, is also the author of *Death, Taxes, and Other Illusions*.

STEVEN HALPERN

♥

"If we are to have peace on our planet, we must experience peace within ourselves."

As a New York born Type-A individual, I was an early candidate for stress burn-out. I didn't like what was happening to my mind, body, and personality, so I began looking for legal, non-addictive, and inexpensive tools and resources to help keep me healthy and in balance. As far back as I can remember, I've always been fascinated by the transcendental power of certain music to bring me to a place of peace and harmony. My early research and graduate studies proved that the healing power of a new form of music I was working with was not an isolated incident. I suddenly realized how I could contribute to my fellow men and women's lives.

In these increasingly stressful times, we all need to take care of ourselves. Medical authorities have documented that one of the best ways that we can maintain our health and well-being is to handle the stress in our lives in an effective manner. Of the many psycho-technologies available for reducing stress, biofeedback, meditation, yoga, and exercise, few are as simple and beautiful as listening to relaxation music. Studies indicate that the "relaxation response" can kick in in a matter of seconds, rather than minutes or hours. Being a Type-A, I found the idea of immediate gratification quite attractive.

Thousands of years after David soothed Saul with his lyre, American culture had essentially forgotten about the healing powers of music. My mission, as I came to understand it, was to reawaken an awareness of the power of sound in our lives. This means addressing issues of noise pollution, as well as assisting individuals to connect with their inner selves and higher power. If we are to have peace on our planet, we must experience peace within ourselves.

Steven Halpern is a composer, recording artist, author, and educator, who is internationally recognized as an authority on the healing power of music. Known as one of the fathers of New Age music, he is a popular speaker and workshop leader who empowers people to hear themselves and their own songs.

HEATHER HUGHES-CALERO

♥

Joy is the compensating principle of balance. When one drops a pebble into a pool of water, its impact spirals outward. So it is when one person finds contentment within himself or herself. Those people become the energy boosters of the world, the carriers of joy, and everyone they meet feels uplifted and encouraged by their presence. How does one achieve a state of contentment and harmony? By learning the art of doing without doing, relaxing with the flow of life, and enjoying the moment.

―♥―

Heather Hughes-Calero is the author of more than a hundred magazine articles and six metaphysical books, including *Writing As a Tool for Self-Discovery, The Sedona Trilogy, The Golden Dream,* and her latest book, *Woman Between the Wind,* an exciting first-hand account of her adventure and training with a Sioux medicine woman. Hughes-Calero's interest in anthropology and dedication to living life through experience caused her to spend many years researching religion and different cultures. During one of her many quests, she worked in Japan with translators, translating the "heart" discourse of the Lotus Sutra from Sanskrit to English. Her exploration in the search for self is expressed in her varied seminars, which have attracted thousands of students from all over the United States.

DALE EVANS

If one person lives up to the light that God has given him or her, that person can contribute greatly to world peace.

When Dale Evans rides into town, any town, thousands upon thousands of people are on hand to cheer and say hello to the Queen of Cowboys. That's because everyone who has ever fancied riding the range knows about Evans and her husband and partner Roy Rogers as the stars of countless rodeos and feature films. They hold nine all-time box office records at the famed Houston Rodeo, including the largest crowd ever to see an indoor rodeo for one performance at the Astrodome—46,884 people!

JOHN W. JAMES & RUSSELL P. FRIEDMAN

"If people are going to make a difference in themselves and the world we live in, we need to learn to allow ourselves and others the dignity to acknowledge and process the sad, painful, and negative feelings that accompany life and significant emotional loss."

We are all familiar with the old ditty that says, "I was unhappy about having no shoes until I met a man who had no feet." If that saying is extended to its obvious conclusion, it implies that there can only be one person entitled to grieve on the planet—the one with the most losses. The unhealthy message here is "compare in order to minimize," something that so many of us do too often.

While we are encouraged to express our happy or positive emotions, we have been socialized to intellectualize our sad or negative emotions. The net effect is that we may have eliminated or hidden half of our emotional range. Millions of people lead limited and restricted lives based on incorrect beliefs on how to respond to and process the normal and natural emotions of life.

If people are going to make a difference in themselves and the world we live in, we need to learn to allow ourselves and others the dignity to acknowledge and process the sad, painful, and negative feelings that accompany life and significant emotional loss. We need to accept, and not be afraid of, our own feelings, good or bad, and then we can learn not to fear the emotions of our friends and loved ones. In fact, we need to encourage the expression of all emotions so that we can grieve our losses, recover from our personal struggles, and complete relationships that have changed or ended. As we create a safe environment for ourselves and others to express all of our emotions, we help reduce the level of fear and apprehension that lead to isolation. As we acknowledge and express our entire range of emotions, we begin to heal. As we heal, we begin to move beyond losses, and retake a productive place in our lives and a renewed interaction with others. It is then that we make a difference.

John W. James is the founder and Russell P. Friedman is the executive director of the Grief Recovery Institute and GRIEF, a nonprofit, public benefit organization in Los Angeles. Recognized by educational organizations across the country, the institute provides Grief Recovery[SM] programs and seminars for grievers and professionals, as well as a national toll-free helpline, and other outreach services. James is the author *The Grief Recovery Handbook,* a step-by-step program for moving beyond loss, and Friedman has pioneered and established over three hundred outreach programs in the United States and Canada.

JENNY CRAIG

♥

When we remind ourselves of the dramatic influence that one man, Jesus Christ, had on Christian people throughout the world, we acknowledge the power of one. If each of us practiced the Ten Commandments and lived a life that would make Him proud, the synergy of our efforts would provide a world with no place for wars, self-destruction, hunger, homelessness, or hatred and injustice to minorities. We would live in a peaceful world filled with love for ourselves and for each other.

―♥―

Jenny Craig is the co-founder and vice chairman of Jenny Craig International, a chain of over 650 company-owned and franchised Weight Loss centers that bear her name. Craig founded her company with her husband Sid in 1983, selecting the then untapped market of Australia. In 1985 Jenny returned to the United States where in just five years the company grew to 650 centers internationally. Her goal is to help as many overweight people "break the cycle of failed diets, [and overcome] feelings of embarrassment, depression, and anxiety."

SUSAN JEFFERS

♥

"... whether in the enclosed space of our home or out in the vastness of the world, every action we take helps determine if this is a world filled with hate and conflict or a world filled with peace and love."

As I look around, I notice that so few of us have the understanding at the deepest level of our beings that our lives make a difference . . . that our actions really do contribute to the pool of energy that defines this world. As a result, the difference we make is too often hurtful instead of healing. It is clear that a change in how we think about ourselves is necessary before we can become a force of love and peace within our families, our communities, and our planet.

We can begin to change our self-perception by playing the game of "act-as-if." That is, with each step of the journey each person asks, "*If* I truly made a difference in this world, what would I be doing? *If* I truly made a difference, how would I be more loving? *If* I truly made a difference, how would I create more harmony around me?"

We then let all our actions come from the answers revealed by our inner wisdom. As you can see, the process is simple, but it requires a lifetime commitment of asking ourselves these important questions, listening for the answers that come from the highest part of who we are, and most importantly, taking the actions that create a healing energy around us. As we consciously and patiently focus on this life-giving game of "act-as-if," we ultimately live into the awesomely wonderful understanding of just how large a difference we can truly make. We learn that, whether in the enclosed space of our home or out in the vastness of the world, every action we take helps determine if this is a world filled with hate and conflict or a world filled with peace and love.

Along the way, we may notice that the lingering pain of past and present hurts can make positive actions difficult. Whenever our hearts are filled with anger and pain, it is difficult, if not impossible, to spread an energy of peace and love onto this earth. At such times, it is empowering for a person to pick up the mirror instead of the magnifying glass and ask, "How can I heal the hurt within? How can I change what doesn't work in my life? How can I transcend to that place where all is love?" And once again, we look to our higher selves to find the answers.

To *know* that we really count is the most powerful and vital piece of information we can have. It introduces a whole new dimension to our being—that of responsibility. A sense of responsibility that comes from a realization of our inner powers is not a burden. It enables us to leave behind our frightened egos and jump to the highest part of who we are. It allows us to create acts of love that make us feel alive and joyful . . . even blissful. At such times, we know we have found our true home . . . that magical place within where we all yearn to dwell. We have only to begin the journey and, with each step forward, we find ourselves a little bit closer to home.

Susan Jeffers, Ph.D., is the author of the best-selling and award-winning book, *Feel the Fear and Do It Anyway*, as well as *Opening Our Hearts to Men, Dare to Connect,* and the forthcoming *The Journey from Lost to Found*. A noted workshop leader, media personality, and speaker, Dr. Jeffers has created numerous audio tapes on the subjects of fear and personal growth.

HARRY CAREY, JR.

We can make the world a better place by doing away with resentment, jealousy, and greed. Love a higher power.

Harry Carey, Jr., is a classic western actor, and has appeared in almost one hundred feature films, including *She Wore A Yellow Ribbon, Rio Grande, Two Rode Together, The Long Riders, Crossroads,* and *Whales of August,* as well as hundreds of television westerns. He is currently at work on a book about his years with "The John Ford Stock Company," a term used for those character actors who consistently appeared in Ford's films.

DENIS WAITLEY

♥

If each person in each middle income family in every developed country in the world ate all that was served at home on each plate of food and served himself or herself only that portion of food that would be eaten and not wasted, the savings in grocery and waste disposal bills would be enough to feed every starving victim of poverty in the world. There will be no peace on earth possible until there is a piece of bread in every mouth. We can demonstrate love and peace best by helping others live, and yes, staying alive. If one parent teaches one child this example in every "have" family, there will be no "have nots" in fifty years.

—♥—

Denis Waitley, Ph.D., is best known as the author and narrator of "The Psychology of Winning" the best-selling audio cassette album on personal and professional development. He also is the author of several national best-selling books, including *Seeds of Greatness, The Winner's Edge,* and *Being the Best.* Dr. Waitley is recognized as an authority on high-level achievement and personal excellence. One of America's most sought after keynote speakers, he has studied and counseled leaders in every field from Superbowl and Olympic athletes to Apollo astronauts and top Fortune 500 corporate executives.

IRVING SARNOFF

By totally committing one's time and energy to the betterment of this world and deciding to *live simply* (small home, cheap car, and minimum purchases of unnecessary material items) each person can make it possible *for others to simply live*. Runaway materialism and egotistical concerns overemphasizing one's individual happiness and well-being are contradictory and hypocritical to spreading love and peace in the world, and the only difference they make is that the conditions on earth get worse.

Irving Sarnoff has been a peace activist and volunteer organizer for the past four decades. He was a founder and director of the Southern California Peace Action Council and the Alliance for Survival. He is vice president of the Southern California World Federalists Association and a founder of Friends of the United Nations. Involved at the national and international levels of peace and anti-nuclear movements, he has attended conferences worldwide on these issues and organized many major events to support the United Nations.

KRIYANANDA
(J. DONALD WALTERS)

♥

Most people want to feel that they have some positive impact on the lives of others. To make a difference in the world, however, isn't that beyond the reach of any one person? Is our planet so small that any single influence can have much impact on it?

Maybe so. Yet influences have a way of spreading like ripples in a pond. If an idea can change people's minds, and inspire them sufficiently to change the very way they live, it will have that ripple effect. Alexander the Great didn't do it, but Buddha did. The Renaissance didn't do it, but Jesus did. Yes, it can be done!

How many public figures declaim on behalf of good causes? Yet how many of them significantly change anything? Think of the fads that are embraced by millions, that fade into nonexistence like ocean waves that fade back tracelessly into the vast body of water from which they rose.

The change must come from within ourselves. And it must come from the heights of that inner being. It cannot come from emotion, or opinion, not even from a sincerely held belief. Truth always wins in the end.

There is the story of Billy Sunday, the evangelist, who died. He appeared before the gates of heaven, but Saint Peter told him he couldn't go in since the evangelist's name was not recorded in the book of good deeds. "But what about all those people I converted?" expostulated Mr. Sunday. "And all those people I sent to heaven?" "You may have sent them," Saint Peter replied, "but none have ever arrived!"

There is also the story of Tansen, the chief musician in the court of the great emperor, Akbar.

> The emperor often exclaimed to Tansen, "No one anywhere sings as well as you do!" Tansen replied, "Your majesty, there is one far greater than I: my own teacher." For a long time Akbar dismissed the answer, thinking of it merely as an expression of humility.
>
> After some time, however, he asked Tansen to let him hear his teacher sing. "He would never agree to come to your court, your majesty," Tansen replied. "To hear him, I must take you to him. Nor will he sing if he recognizes you as the emperor. You must go disguised as a common man."
>
> The emperor agreed to go in disguise with Tansen. The teacher, however, though glad to see his pupil again, refused to sing for his supposed friend. Finally, Tansen tricked his teacher by singing a melody he had learned in his student days, deliberately making a mistake in what he'd learned. At this point, what could the teacher do but correct his pupil? He sang the melody as it should have been sung.
>
> The emperor was astounded. When they left, he exclaimed, "You were right! I never imagined a human being could sing with such a heavenly voice. How is it that you, whose singing seems humanly perfect, hasn't the power to perform with such sublimity?"
>
> "Your majesty," replied Tansen, "the difference is simply this. I sing to please you, but my teacher sings only to please God."

To make a difference, then, we should serve no one but God and truth. Anything less will be but a wave. It may rise for a time, but very soon it will sink again and be forgotten.

———❤———

Kriyananda is a man of international outlook, reputation, and upbringing. Educated in Rumania, Switzerland, England, India, and the United States, Kriyananda has lectured throughout the world, and is the author of some thirty "how to live" books, the latest of which is entitled *The Essence of Self-Realization: The Wisdom of Paramhansa Yogananda.* Kriyananda is a direct disciple of Paramhansa Yogananda, with whom he lived the last three and a half years of the master's life. Head of Yogananda's male monastic order and lecturer of Yogananda's teachings, Kriyananda is the founder of the Ananda World Brotherhood Village, dedicated to cooperative spiritual living.

ANTHONY ROBBINS

♥

What creates a lasting sense of fulfillment? For over a decade, I've had the unique privilege of working with people from virtually all walks of life, from the privileged to the impoverished. One thing stands clear: Regardless of stature, only those who have learned the power of sincere and selfless contribution experience life's deepest joy—true fulfillment. We all respect those who consistently give of themselves. Life is a gift, and all of us who have the capacity must remember that we have the responsibility to give something back. Discover and demonstrate your unlimited capacity to care. Make a difference in the world.

―♥―

A millionaire by the age of twenty-four, Anthony Robbins is an entrepreneur, the founder of nine companies, and author of the best-selling *Awakening the Power Within* and *Unlimited Power,* a book now published in eleven languages around the world. Considered one of the nation's leaders in human development training, he is the founder and president of Robbins Research International, Inc., the research and marketing arm of his personal development businesses. Robbins has established The Anthony Robbins Foundation as a philanthropic organization dedicated to assisting those individuals who would not otherwise be reached—the nation's youth, elderly, homeless, and prison population.

PETER J. DANIELS

Peace is more than the absence of war. It is the opportunity for a human being to grow within the confines of the laws of God, but most of all, the rights of others. Peace is not the quantity of fulfillment, but an open door to acquisition. Peace sometimes needs to be defended from greed, power holders, and bullies which, unfortunately, means that in the defense, humankind exhibits the worst in an effort to redeem the best. Peace and love are the opportunity to give under the banner of Jesus Christ.

Peter J. Daniels is a millionaire land developer, one of Australia's top motivational speakers, and a Christian. As a speaker lecturing internationally and throughout Australia on real estate, leadership, management, and goal setting, Daniels's lectures are spiced with biblical principles for living. He is the author of *How to Reach Your Life Goals* and *How to Be Happy Though Rich,* a testimony and guide for others to Christian principles.

DICK VAN PATTEN

♥

Give of yourself to others and the love will come back tenfold.

Dick Van Patten is best known for his role on the television series, "Eight Is Enough." A veteran actor, Van Patten has been in seven television series, twenty-four feature films, and twenty-seven Broadway plays.

JOSE SILVA

♥

"All we need to do is to learn to correct problems and achieve our goals by using positive, creative, and constructive means, rather than negative, destructive means."

Can one individual make a difference in the world? Can one person actually do anything to help bring peace to our planet? The answer is definitely yes. And I have a formula to make it happen. The formula I have used for years is this: 1 + 2 = 5 billion. What do I mean by that? I mean that if each person influences just two other people, and each of those two influences just two people, then soon all 5 billion humans on the planet will get the message.

SPREAD THE WORD

What message do people need to hear, in order to bring peace to our planet? People need to learn that they can get whatever they need to be successful, healthy, prosperous, and happy, without taking things away from other people, and without hurting other people.

When people learn to center themselves brain frequency-wise, to function at the center of the brain frequency spectrum so that they can use both brain hemispheres to think with, then they will be able to get help from the other side, to solve problems on this side, in the physical dimension. We need to let people know that there is a method for them to do this. People can learn to actually enter the alpha level with conscious awareness so that they can think with either the logical left brain hemisphere, or the creative and intuitive right brain hemisphere, to gain more insight, obtain more information, and thereby correct more problems.

REAP THE HARVEST

There is enough of everything in the world for everybody. All we need to do is to learn to correct problems and achieve our goals by using positive, creative, and constructive means, rather than negative, destructive means. I believe that we were put here by the creator to help correct problems and to convert the planet into a paradise. It makes no sense to see people destroying each other in the name of the creator. We can create a paradise on earth if we so desire.

I'm not the first to suggest that. There have been many great religious leaders who have said the same thing, each in his or her own way. All of these religious leaders were correct in the things that they said. They were all seeking to help people, to lead them in the correct direction. It is their followers that we need to watch out for. All too often, the followers misunderstand the message of their leader, and as a result, they create conflict.

Why do the followers misunderstand? Because they are not centered. They do not know how to center themselves so that they can use both brain hemispheres to think with, and get help from the other side. Because the followers are not centered, they observe things from a different perspective than their leaders. The leaders are centered. They have access to information from the other side, from higher intelligence, from God. The followers, though, are not centered and thus are limited to their own thoughts and feelings and prejudices and misconceptions and false information.

WHAT YOU MUST DO

When you learn to center yourself and see things from a higher perspective, then you function like the leaders of the great religions; you become one who creates rather than destroys; you become a creator, a creator of paradise on this planet. How can you know when you are able to obtain information with your mind, information that is not available to your physical senses, and then verify that this information is correct?

Intuition is a faculty of the mind. The better your intuition is, the more effective you are in the mental and spiritual dimension. When you know that you are able to use your mind to get information and use this information to correct problems, then you will begin to create your own paradise, without hurting anyone else, without taking anything from anyone else. When you do this, other people will want to learn how to do the same thing.

BE A PEACEMAKER

If you will make sure that just two people learn how to center themselves and function in this manner, and each of those people spread the word to just two more people, we can soon bring peace to our planet. Let's spread the word to everyone. Let's get everyone centered, and humanize humanity. 1 + 2 = 5 billion. Let's make it happen.

Jose Silva is the founder of the Silva Mind Control Method, a system of mental training that has millions of exponents worldwide. A blend of dynamic meditation, relaxation, auto-suggestion, and positive thinking, it has been taught in American schools to improve students' IQs. Silva holds a doctor's award in humanities and is the chairman of four corporations.

LYNN ANDREWS

Perfection in life has to do with walking in balance with a foot in the physical world and a foot always in the spirit. If a person can truly live with that balance in his or her life, a deep sisterhood and brotherhood is formed between all cultures, races, and sexes throughout the world. You begin to explore one of the first lessons of power—that we are all alone. The last lesson of power then becomes a realization of the heart that we are all one.

A shaman and preeminent teacher in the field of personal development, Lynn Andrews made her mark as a *New York Times* best-selling author, and has gained worldwide following since her first book, *Medicine Woman,* was published in 1981. She has chronicled her incredible journeys into self-discovery and enlightenment in eight books, including *The Woman of Wyrrd,* and in *The Power Deck: The Cards of Wisdom,* a meditation and affirmation deck described in *The Woman of Wyrrd*. Her life and work are devoted to healing the planet by first healing the individual.

INDEX

Alireza, Marianne, 47
Allen, Pat, 77-78
Allen, Robert, 19
Andrews, Lynn, 156
Arrien, Angeles, 7-8
Asner, Ed, 18
Bethards, Betty, 87-89
Bishop, Joey, 37
Blanchard, Kenneth, 48
Branden, Nathaniel, 9-10
Canfield, Jack, 64-66
Carey, Jr., Harry, 142
Cole-Whittaker, Terry, 20-21
Coté, Christine Bingham, 126-128
Coté, Paul, 49-51
Craig, Jenny, 138
Daniels, Peter, 151
Davenport, Rita, 79-80
De Angelis, Barbara, 93-96
Dees, Rick, 62-63
Dheming, Korey, 73-75
Eichberg, Rob, 44-46
Evans, Dale, 135
Friedman, Russell, 136-137
Gawain, Shakti, 119-121
Gillies, Jerry, 103-104
Greene, Richard, 81-84
Gunther, Bernard, 61
Halpern, Steven, 131-132
Hansen, Mark Victor, 85-86
Hawkins, Jimmy, 24-25
Hay, Louise L., 69-71
Hilton, Kathy, 105
Hope, Bob, 55
Houston, Jean, 56-58
Hughes-Calero, Heather, 133-134
Iacocca, Lee, 90
James, John W., 136-137

Jampolsky, Gerald, 13-15
Jeffers, Susan, 139-141
Jones, Charles T., 26-28
Justin, Thomas H., 113-115
Kasem, Casey, 97-98
Kennedy, Danielle, 29-30
Keyes, Ken, 11-12
King, Serge Kahili, 35-36
Kriyananda, 146-148
Leach, Robin, 72
Martin, Dean, 99
McMahon, Ed, 31
Millman, Dan, 40-43
Moss, Richard, 52-53
Norton, Ken, 112
O'Leary, Brian, 16-17
Orr, Leonard, 111
Patent, Arnold, 129-130
Ray, Sondra, 22-23
Reese, Della, 100-102
Rhodes, Frank H.T., 125
Robbins, Anthony, 149-150
Sams, Jamie, 116-118
Sarnoff, Irving, 145
Schaef, Anne Wilson, 38-39
Schuller, Robert A., 32-34
Silva, Jose, 153-155
Stafford, Susan Carney, 67-68
Steinberg, Leigh, 59-60
Tracy, Brian, 123-124
Van Derbur, Marilyn, 54
Van Patten, Dick, 152
Vasconcellos, John, 91-92
Waitley, Denis, 143-144
Weaver, Dennis, 122
Willit, Boyd, 76
Zukav, Gary, 106-110

ABOUT THE AUTHOR

♥

Danielle Marie is a successful entrepreneur with a background in sales consulting and negotiating. An experienced public speaker, Marie has always been involved in making a difference in the world. This North Dakota native grew up in a family who taught her the importance of giving. She has been a foster mother, an Action volunteer, and has worked with various charitable organizations. She makes her home in Southern California.

ORDER FORM

♥

**CONTACT:
National Book Network
4720 Boston Way
Lanham, MD 20706
1-800-462-6420**
Visa and Mastercard accepted.

---

*Pure Wisdom:
Insight for Those Seeking Happiness
and Peace of Mind* — $10.95

*The Spiritual Seeker's Guide:
The Complete Source for Religions and
Spiritual Groups of the World* — $12.95

*Straight from the Heart:
Authors, Celebrities & Others Share
Their Philosophies on Making a Difference
in the World* — $10.95